Apress Pocket Guides

Apress Pocket Guides present concise summaries of cutting-edge developments and working practices throughout the tech industry. Shorter in length, books in this series aims to deliver quick-to-read guides that are easy to absorb, perfect for the time-poor professional.

This series covers the full spectrum of topics relevant to the modern industry, from security, AI, machine learning, cloud computing, web development, product design, to programming techniques and business topics too.

Typical topics might include:

- A concise guide to a particular topic, method, function or framework

- Professional best practices and industry trends

- A snapshot of a hot or emerging topic

- Industry case studies

- Concise presentations of core concepts suited for students and those interested in entering the tech industry

- Short reference guides outlining 'need-to-know' concepts and practices.

More information about this series at `https://link.springer.com/bookseries/17385`.

SQL in a Week

A Fast-Track Guide to Writing
and Optimizing Queries
Like a Pro

Bhumika Shah
Devtosh Dubey

Apress®

SQL in a Week: A Fast-Track Guide to Writing and Optimizing Queries Like a Pro

Bhumika Shah
Milford, USA

Devtosh Dubey
Milford, USA

ISBN-13 (pbk): 979-8-8688-2101-1
https://doi.org/10.1007/979-8-8688-2102-8

ISBN-13 (electronic): 979-8-8688-2102-8

Managing Director, Apress Media LLC: Welmoed Spahr
Acquisitions Editor: Shaul Elson
Development Editor: Laura Berendson
Coordinating Editor: Gryffin Winkler

Cover image designed by eStudioCalamar

Distributed to the book trade worldwide by Springer Science+Business Media New York, 1 New York Plaza, New York, NY 10004. Phone 1-800-SPRINGER, fax (201) 348-4505, e-mail orders-ny@springer-sbm.com, or visit www.springeronline.com. Apress Media, LLC is a Delaware LLC and the sole member (owner) is Springer Science + Business Media Finance Inc (SSBM Finance Inc). SSBM Finance Inc is a **Delaware** corporation.

For information on translations, please e-mail booktranslations@springernature.com; for reprint, paperback, or audio rights, please e-mail bookpermissions@springernature.com.

Apress titles may be purchased in bulk for academic, corporate, or promotional use. eBook versions and licenses are also available for most titles. For more information, reference our Print and eBook Bulk Sales web page at http://www.apress.com/bulk-sales.

Any source code or other supplementary material referenced by the author in this book is available to readers on GitHub. For more detailed information, please visit https://www.apress.com/gp/services/source-code.

If disposing of this product, please recycle the paper

Table of Contents

About the Authors

 **Bhumika Shah** is an accomplished engineer, PhD scholar, speaker, and educator, specializing in AI, Data Engineering, and Information Governance. With over seven years of experience, she has designed scalable data pipelines, strengthened data governance frameworks, and developed AI-driven predictive models that improve efficiency across industries. Her work has been published in peer-reviewed journals, and she is a strong advocate for leveraging AI and data engineering to enhance regulatory compliance and operational performance. She believes that data is a powerful asset—when utilized effectively, it can transform decision-making, drive innovation, and create lasting impact for businesses.

Bhumika has successfully aced over a dozen technical interviews at global companies, including MAANG firms, giving her first-hand insight into the SQL skills required to excel in real-world data roles. She has designed and taught graduate-level courses in Data Management and Analytics as a professor, equipping students with practical expertise in SQL, data governance, and cloud-based data engineering. She also actively mentors master's degree students, helping them bridge the gap between academic theory and industry best practices.

Currently pursuing a PhD in Information Technology with a focus on exploring the impact of AI on data teams, Bhumika continues to advance research in big data analytics, business intelligence, and AI applications.

Bhumika believes SQL is a critical skill for professionals working with data, as it enables them to retrieve accurate information and transform it into actionable insights. She also emphasizes that SQL isn't just about writing queries, but it's about writing *optimized* queries that unlock efficiency and create real business impact.

Devtosh Dubey is a results-driven Senior Business Data Analyst with extensive experience in designing scalable data solutions, performing advanced statistical analyses, and leading cross-functional teams to deliver data-driven insights. With a strong PySpark, SQL, and statistical modeling background, Devtosh has optimized ETL pipelines and analytical workflows, significantly enhancing operational efficiency and supporting strategic business decisions. He has spearheaded high-impact analytical projects across healthcare and technology sectors, enabling targeted user segmentation, predictive modeling, and KPI-driven dashboard development. His work has contributed directly to revenue growth, client satisfaction, and streamlined data operations.

Devtosh is also experienced in developing production-grade dashboards, managing curated audience segmentation, and reducing data latency through efficient integration strategies. His technical toolkit includes Python, SQL, Tableau, Power BI, and AWS Redshift, with proficiency in tools such as Pandas, SciPy, and Scikit-learn. He thrives in collaborative environments, is adept at mentoring colleagues, working with external partners, and translating complex data into actionable insights that support business objectives.

About the Technical Reviewer

Sreeni Bhogireddy is a Data Engineering and Business Intelligence professional with over 15 years of experience designing and delivering scalable data solutions that transform complex data into meaningful business insights. His expertise spans modern data platforms and BI ecosystems including Databricks, Snowflake, Azure Data Factory (ADF), Informatica Intelligent Cloud Services (IICS), SQL, Python, PySpark, Apache Airflow, and Data Modeling, along with visualization tools such as Tableau, Power BI, and SAP Business Objects.

Throughout his career, Sreeni has led critical data initiatives across multiple domains including Healthcare (Epic Clarity and Caboodle), Supply Chain (Order Management, Planning, and Fulfillment), and Finance. He specializes in building end-to-end data pipelines, optimizing data architectures, and developing high-performance analytical solutions that enable organizations to make data-driven decisions.

Sreeni's work focuses on improving operational efficiency, optimizing reporting performance, and delivering scalable data platforms that support enterprise analytics. He has successfully mentored junior developers, led cross-functional data projects, and aligned technical data solutions with broader business strategy to deliver measurable outcomes.

Acknowledgments

This book would not have been possible without the patience, encouragement, and belief of the people around us. To the students and professionals who trusted us with their SQL questions, thank you for being the spark behind this project. Your curiosity showed us where learning gets hard and reminded us why making it easier matters. We are especially grateful to the learners and professionals who shared their SQL frustrations and successes with us over the years. Their experiences shaped the examples, scenarios, and teaching approach within these pages.

We owe a special debt of gratitude to our parents, **Mr. Raj Kumar Shah, Mrs. Preety Shah, Dr. Monika Dubey, and Dr. Ashutosh Kumar Dubey,** for their love, belief, and unwavering support throughout this journey. Thank you for giving us the confidence to build, to teach, and to complete work we are truly proud of.

Introduction

In today's data-driven world, the ability to speak SQL is no longer a niche skill—it's a career advantage. Whether you're a data analyst preparing for interviews, a product manager trying to pull reports from a database, or a VP who wants to challenge assumptions with evidence, this book is for you. You don't need a computer science degree. You don't need prior coding experience. You need a structured, step-by-step guide that gets you from beginner to confident in one week. Even in the age of AI, where tools can auto-generate queries, understanding how SQL works gives you a real edge. You'll be able to ask more thoughtful questions, validate results, and avoid being misled by automation. AI can suggest syntax, but you bring the context, the logic, and the decision-making power.

As data professionals who have worked in high-pressure industries for years, cracked interviews at Amazon and Meta, and taught SQL to hundreds of graduate students and professionals, we authors know what works—and what doesn't. This book doesn't overload you with theory. It teaches what matters in the real world—from writing your first SELECT query to optimizing performance like a pro. Every chapter builds on the last, so you can practice, progress, and retain what you learn. At the end of every chapter, you'll find Key Takeaways highlighting concepts you learned that day, best practices of the day, common mistakes to avoid, and how each topic keeps you relevant in the AI era—because knowing how and why SQL works matters more than ever. By the end of seven days, you'll be able to read, write, and debug SQL confidently—whether in a strategy meeting, product design session, or tech interview.

This book takes you on a journey toward data fluency. No jargon. No fluff. Just powerful, practical SQL. The chapters are concise and focused, designed to build a strong foundation for our readers. In 2026 and beyond, almost anyone with this foundational knowledge can leverage SQL to support informed business decisions. Over the next seven days, this book will help you move from beginner to confident SQL user—not just writing queries, but writing them correctly.

Getting Started/First Steps

Before you write your first line of SQL (Structured Query Language), let's understand what SQL is—and why it's one of the most valuable tools in the digital age.

SQL is used to communicate with relational databases. Whether you're working in healthcare, marketing, finance, or tech, most data is stored in a relational database. SQL is the language used to retrieve, insert, update, and delete data. As humans use English to communicate with the world, you can use SQL to communicate with databases.

SQL is Declarative, which means the user can state what they want (not how to get it). SQL is Universal, i.e., almost every major organization relies on SQL-based systems, and SQL is Powerful since you can explore millions of records with a few lines of SQL.

SQL basic concepts and its role in relational databases will be explored in greater depth in Chapter 1 of this book, but think of a relational database as an organized digital filing cabinet. Inside are tables that store your data, like spreadsheets, but smarter. Each table has rows (records) and columns (fields). Example: A "Customers" table might have columns like "CustomerID," "Name," "Email," and "Country," and each row contains data for one customer.

Relational databases like MySQL, PostgreSQL, SQL Server, and Oracle follow structured rules that allow data to be connected and queried efficiently.

Key SQL Building Blocks

Before you dive into querying, here are some basic concepts you'll work with throughout this book (see Figure 1):

Tables: Store data in rows and columns.

Rows: Represent a single record.

Columns: Represent a specific type of information (e.g., name, date).

Primary Key: A unique identifier for each row.

Foreign Key: A field in one table that links to the primary key in another.

Data Types: Define the type of data a column can hold (e.g., "INT," "VARCHAR," "DATE").

Schema: The blueprint of your database—how tables are structured and related.

Relationships connect tables using keys—this allows data to stay organized and consistent (like how your lover needs the key to your heart to stay in the relationship).

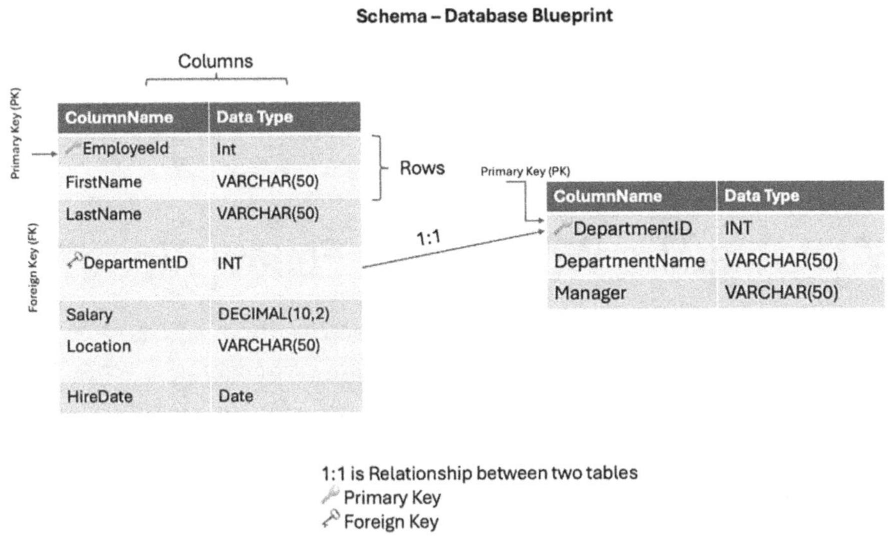

Schema – Database Blueprint

Figure 1. *Schema—Database blueprint*

How SQL Fits into the Real World?

You don't have to be a software developer to benefit from SQL. If you're

Product Managers:

Stop waiting on analysts. With basic SQL, you can query customer data yourself and make faster, data-driven decisions.

Business Analysts:

SQL is your core tool. It helps you clean, transform, and extract insights from data efficiently.

VPs and Executives:

Dashboards are great, but knowing simple SQL lets you verify numbers and dig deeper when speed matters.

Students and Job Seekers:

SQL is a must-have for any data role. Strong SQL
skills can set you apart in interviews and on the job.

What Readers Will Need to Follow Along?

To start learning SQL with this book, you'll need a simple and easy-to-use
SQL environment—and that's where SQLite comes in. SQLite is a free,
beginner-friendly database tool that lets you practice SQL without any
complex setup. To help you get started, this book comes with a step-by-
step setup instruction guide. Just follow along to download and install the
software from `https://sqlitebrowser.org`, choose the right version for
your system (Windows or Mac), and complete the installation. With your
tools ready, you'll be all set to begin your SQL journey—no experience
needed. You'll need a curious mindset and willingness to experiment.

This book will walk you through every step. Starting Sunday, let's build
your foundation and prepare for your first real SQL query!

Hang Tight! Your New Journey Begins

To make this learning experience more relatable and engaging, imagine
yourself as the newly appointed CEO of DataNova Corp—a fast-
growing startup with a team of 10 employees spread across the globe.
Your workforce includes developers, marketers, analysts, and support staff
in cities like New York, London, Bangalore, and Tokyo. You've inherited
a basic employee database containing names, departments, salaries,
locations, and start dates. Your mission? Use SQL to uncover insights,
drive intelligent business decisions, and confidently lead your company.
Each chapter in this book builds upon this evolving story, starting today by
helping you understand who's on your team.

Setup Instructions: Getting Ready to Learn SQL

To follow along with this book, you'll need a working SQL environment. We'll use **SQLite**—a free, powerful tool that's widely used in the industry.

Step 1: Download and Install SQLite

1. For the purposes of this book, we will be working with the SQLite Database.

2. Go to `https://sqlitebrowser.org`, head to the download section in the top menu.

3. Download the package based on your PC (Mac, Windows).

4. Run the software, and the installation process should go smoothly.

Note You may also need **SQL Server Express Edition** if no database engine is currently installed on your system. It's also free and available on the Microsoft website.

Step 2: Open DB Browser and Create Your Own Database

1. Launch DB Browser for SQLite.

2. Click New Database.

- Choose a location on your computer where you want to create the Database.

- Give your Database a name in the Save As field (mysqlweek).

Step 3: Create Required Tables and Seed Data

Once you hit save, a dialog box opens prompting you to create a table.

"X" out the dialog box and run the following commands individually by pressing Cmd or Ctrl plus the Enter key.

Run the following SQL script to set up all the required tables and insert basic sample data:

```sql
-- CREATE TABLES

-- 1. Employees Table (uses DepartmentID now)
CREATE TABLE Employees (
    EmployeeID   INT PRIMARY KEY,
    FirstName    VARCHAR(50),
    LastName     VARCHAR(50),
    DepartmentID INT,
    Salary       DECIMAL(10,2),
    Location     VARCHAR(50),
    HireDate     DATE,
    FOREIGN KEY (DepartmentID) REFERENCES
Departments(DepartmentID)
);

-- 2. Departments Table
CREATE TABLE Departments (
    DepartmentID   INT PRIMARY KEY,
```

```sql
    DepartmentName VARCHAR(50),
    Manager        VARCHAR(50)
);

-- 3. Projects Table
CREATE TABLE Projects (
    ProjectID   INT PRIMARY KEY,
    ProjectName VARCHAR(100),
    DepartmentID INT,
    Budget      DECIMAL(12,2),
    StartDate   DATE,
    FOREIGN KEY (DepartmentID) REFERENCES
Departments(DepartmentID)
);

-- 4. Assignments Table (Many-to-Many)
CREATE TABLE Assignments (
    EmployeeID   INT,
    ProjectID    INT,
    Role         VARCHAR(50),
    HoursPerWeek INT,
    PRIMARY KEY (EmployeeID, ProjectID),
    FOREIGN KEY (EmployeeID) REFERENCES Employees(EmployeeID),
    FOREIGN KEY (ProjectID) REFERENCES Projects(ProjectID)
);

-- INSERTING DATA IN DEPARTMENTS TABLE
INSERT INTO Departments (DepartmentID, DepartmentName, Manager)
VALUES
    (1, 'Marketing', 'Laura Diaz'),
    (2, 'Engineering', 'Sam Patel'),
    (3, 'HR', 'Tina Chen'),
    (4, 'Support', 'Rajiv Nair');
```

```sql
--INSERTING DATA IN EMPLOYEES TABLE
INSERT INTO Employees (EmployeeID, FirstName, LastName,
DepartmentID, Salary, Location, HireDate)
VALUES
    (1, 'Alice',   'Johnson', 1,  72000.00, 'New York',
    '2021-04-01'),
    (2, 'Bob',     'Lee',     2,  95000.00, 'San Francisco',
    '2020-01-15'),
    (3, 'Carlos', 'Ramirez', 3,  65000.00,
    'London',          '2019-09-30'),
    (4, 'Diana',  'Wang',    4,  60000.00, 'Bangalore',
    '2022-06-10'),
    (5, 'Ethan',  'Kim',     2,  98000.00, 'Seoul',
    '2018-11-12'),
    (6, 'Fiona',  'Davis',   1,  71000.00, 'New York',
    '2022-02-01'),
    (7, 'George', 'Clark',   2, 105000.00, 'San Francisco',
    '2017-03-20'),
    (8, 'Hannah', 'Zhang',   3,  67000.00, 'London',
    '2020-07-18'),
    (9, 'Ivan',   'Petrov',  4,  59000.00, 'Bangalore',
    '2021-10-25'),
    (10,'Jenny',  'Nguyen',  2,  97000.00, 'Tokyo',
    '2019-12-03');

--INSERTING DATA IN Projects TABLE
INSERT INTO Projects (ProjectID, ProjectName, DepartmentID,
Budget, StartDate)
VALUES
    (101, 'Brand Redesign',     1, 150000.00, '2023-01-01'),
    (102, 'AI Chatbot',         2, 300000.00, '2022-07-15'),
    (103, 'Recruitment Drive',  3,  80000.00, '2022-11-20'),
```

```
    (104, 'Helpdesk Upgrade',      4,  60000.00, '2023-04-10'),
    (105, 'Product Launch',        1, 200000.00, '2023-05-01'),
    (106, 'Cloud Migration',       2, 400000.00, '2021-09-10'),
    (107, 'Employee Onboarding',   3,  95000.00, '2022-03-15'),
    (108, 'Ticket System Revamp',  4,  75000.00, '2023-06-01');

-- Assignments
INSERT INTO Assignments (EmployeeID, ProjectID, Role,
HoursPerWeek)
VALUES
    (1,   101, 'Coordinator',       10),
    (2,   102, 'Developer',         20),
    (3,   103, 'HR Lead',           15),
    (4,   104, 'Support Agent',     25),
    (5,   102, 'AI Engineer',       30),
    (6,   105, 'Marketing Analyst', 12),
    (7,   106, 'Cloud Architect',   25),
    (8,   107, 'Trainer',           18),
    (9,   108, 'IT Support',        20),
    (10,  106, 'DevOps Engineer',   28),
    (1,   105, 'Content Creator',   10),
    (2,   106, 'Lead Engineer',     15);

-- Create Table Timesheets
CREATE TABLE Timesheets (
    EmployeeID  INT             NOT NULL,
    ProjectID   INT             NOT NULL,
    WeekStart   DATE            NOT NULL,
    Hours       DECIMAL(5, 2)   NOT NULL,
    FOREIGN KEY (EmployeeID) REFERENCES Employees(EmployeeID)
);
```

```sql
-- Insert Values in Timesheets table
INSERT INTO Timesheets (EmployeeID, ProjectID, WeekStart, Hours)
VALUES
    (1,  101, '2023-06-05', 10),
    (1,  105, '2023-06-05', 12),
    (2,  102, '2023-06-05', 18),
    (2,  106, '2023-06-05', 15),
    (5,  102, '2023-06-05', 30),
    (7,  106, '2023-06-05', 22),
    (10, 106, '2023-06-05', 25),
    (9,  108, '2023-06-05', 20),
    (1,  101, '2023-06-12',  8),
    (1,  105, '2023-06-12', 10),
    (2,  102, '2023-06-12', 20),
    (2,  106, '2023-06-12', 12),
    (5,  102, '2023-06-12', 28),
    (7,  106, '2023-06-12', 25),
    (10, 106, '2023-06-12', 28),
    (9,  108, '2023-06-12', 18);

--- Create Table SalaryChanges
CREATE TABLE SalaryChanges (
    EmployeeID    INT             NOT NULL,
    EffectiveDate DATE            NOT NULL,
    NewSalary     DECIMAL(10, 2)  NOT NULL,
    FOREIGN KEY (EmployeeID) REFERENCES Employees(EmployeeID)
);

INSERT INTO SalaryChanges (EmployeeID, EffectiveDate, NewSalary)
-- Insert Values into SalaryChanges
VALUES
    (1, '2022-01-01',  68000.00),
    (1, '2023-04-01',  72000.00),
```

xxx

```
(2, '2020-01-15',  90000.00),
(2, '2022-08-01',  95000.00),
(5, '2019-11-12',  92000.00),
(5, '2022-05-01',  98000.00),
(7, '2018-01-01',  99000.00),
(7, '2021-03-01', 105000.00);
```

You're Ready!

Your Database is now set up and populated with realistic data to support all seven days of SQL week learning. You can also view the tables by navigating to the Database Structure Tab, and make sure to refresh the Database to view the tables you just created. Happy coding!!!! Let's dive into Sunday!

CHAPTER 1

Sunday: Introduction to SQL—The Language of Data

Goal: Sundays are for slow mornings, second cups of coffee, and setting the tone for the week ahead. And in this book, Sunday is a launchpad into the world of data, with SQL as your trusty sidekick. The goal for today is to introduce SQL as the foundation of working with data, explain what relational databases are, and guide you through setting up your environment and writing your first SQL query. We will also explore SQL data types and why they are important.

What Is SQL, and Why Is It So Important?

SQL is the language of **relational databases;** the systems that store and manage data for nearly every industry—finance, healthcare, retail, tech, education, and beyond. Anytime you check your bank balance, book a flight, or view your health records, SQL is probably working in the background.

Think of SQL as a way to **communicate with your database (like English is used in many countries to communicate with humans)**—you write a query, and the database responds with the answer. For example:

© Bhumika Shah and Devtosh Dubey 2026
B. Shah and D. Dubey, *SQL in a Week*, Apress Pocket Guides,
https://doi.org/10.1007/979-8-8688-2102-8_1

Example 1

```
SELECT * FROM Employees WHERE Location = 'Tokyo';
```

This simple command tells the database: "Show all employees working from Tokyo." And the output will look like this:

	EmployeeID	FirstName	LastName	DepartmentID	Salary	Location	HireDate
1	10	Jenny	Nguyen	2	97000	Tokyo	2019-12-03

Example 2

```
SELECT * FROM Departments WHERE DepartmentName = 'HR';
```

This simple command tells the database: "Show everything in department table where department name is HR."

	DepartmentID	DepartmentName	Manager
1	3	HR	Tina Chen

Tip   Think of SQL functions as if you're speaking in English—*"Show me these details, from this place, but only if certain conditions are met."* The SELECT command chooses what details you want, i.e., columns you want; the FROM command points to where the data lives, i.e., tables where these columns are; and the WHERE command narrows it down with conditions, i.e., data filtering. Easy, right?

SQL isn't just about extracting data—it allows you to **filter, sort, update, analyze, and optimize** how data is retrieved and managed. You will learn more about how to use these SQL features step by step in the upcoming chapters.

Understanding Relational Databases

At the heart of SQL is the **relational database**—a structured collection of tables that relate to one another.

Let's break that down:

- A **table** is like a spreadsheet with rows and columns.

- Each **row** is a record (like a single person or product).

- Each **column** is a field (like name, age, or price).

- **Relationships** connect tables using keys—this allows data to stay organized and consistent (similar to how your lover needs the key to your heart to stay in the relationship). *Keep this word key in mind! We will talk about Foreign key and Primary key later.*

For example:

In Figure 1-1, the Employee table might connect to a department table through a shared key, "DepartmentID", and each employee can have an association with one department, i.e., 1:N relation.

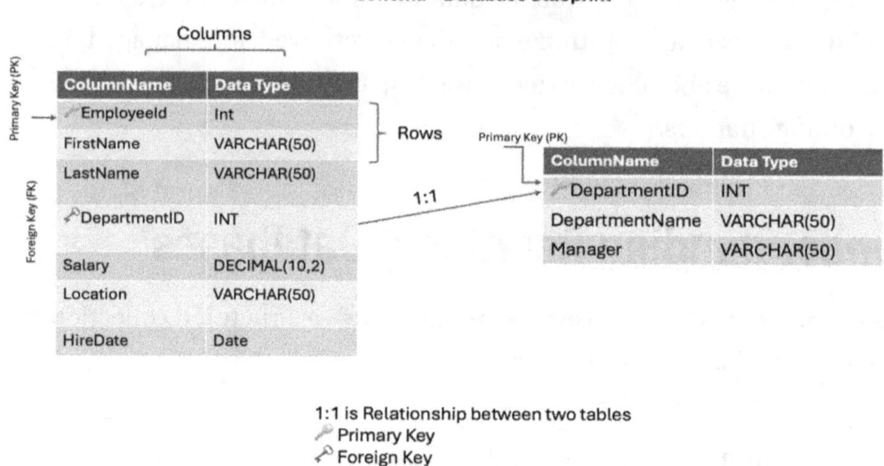

Figure 1-1. *Database Blueprint*

Setting Up Your SQL Environment

Before we write our first query, let's set up your workspace. You can use SQLite for simplicity—it's lightweight and doesn't require a server.

- Download DB Browser for SQLite (`https:// sqlitebrowser.org/dl/`)—it's free and user-friendly.

  - When you click the link, you will get redirected to the website as shown in Figure 1-2.

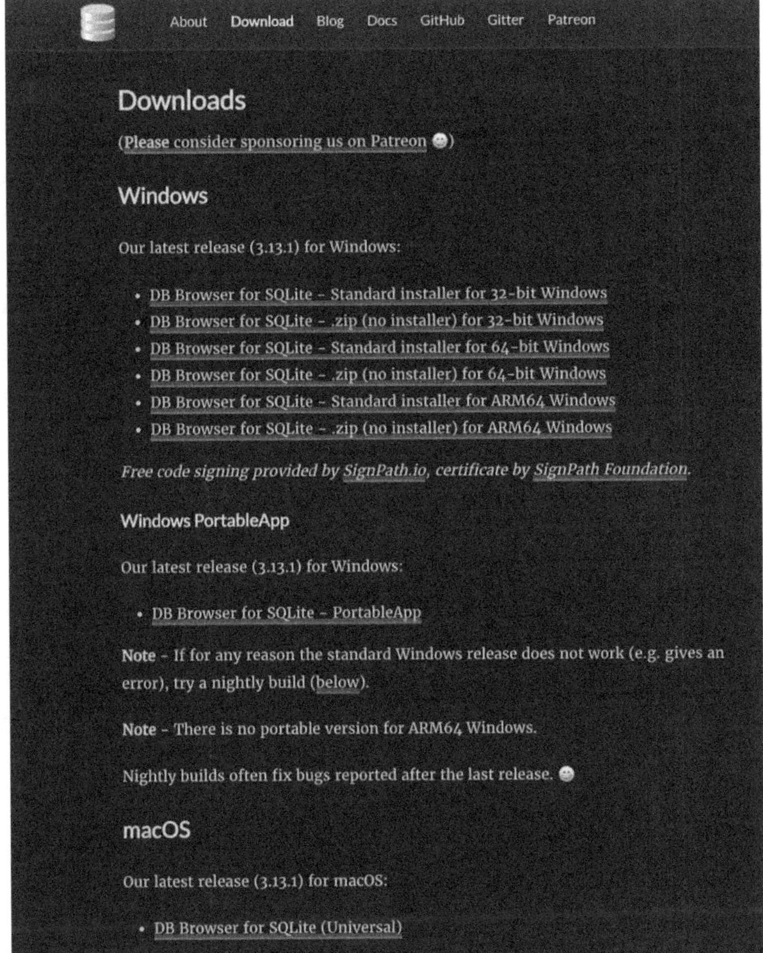

Figure 1-2. *DB Browser for SQLite Interface*

- Once you are on the website, download the version that fits your system requirements.

- Follow setup instructions: `https://docs.google.com/document/d/1caDUwL4MOjYmBzTT86dmFIvjYAjaOoun/edit`.

Your First SQL Query

Let's first understand—"What is a Query?"

A **query** is a set of instructions; you give a database to get specific information. It's like asking a question, and the database gives you the answer using your data. So, in the previous example, SELECT * FROM Employees WHERE Location = 'Tokyo' is SQL Query.

It has SQL commands and instructs database to produce output for all employees located in Tokyo.

Now, let's jump in with a basic query. Suppose we have a table called Employees.

Try this:

```
SELECT * FROM Employees;
```

This command tells the database: "Show me everything in the Employees table."

Learn what's happening:

SELECT => the command to retrieve data **_(Keyword)_**

* => all columns **_(Expression)_**

FROM => where to get the data **_(Keyword)_**

Employees => the name of the table **_(Table Identifier)_**

This query will produce the output in Figure 1-3.

	EmployeeID	FirstName	LastName	DepartmentID	Salary	Location	HireDate
1	1	Alice	Johnson	1	72000	New York	2021-04-01
2	2	Bob	Lee	2	95000	San Francisco	2020-01-15
3	3	Carlos	Ramirez	3	65000	London	2019-09-30
4	4	Diana	Wang	4	60000	Bangalore	2022-06-10
5	5	Ethan	Kim	2	98000	Seoul	2018-11-12
6	6	Fiona	Davis	1	71000	New York	2022-02-01
7	7	George	Clark	2	105000	San Francisco	2017-03-20
8	8	Hannah	Zhang	3	67000	London	2020-07-18
9	9	Ivan	Petrov	4	59000	Bangalore	2021-10-25
10	10	Jenny	Nguyen	2	97000	Tokyo	2019-12-03

Figure 1-3. *Query Output*

Now, let's take another example. Let's check all the departments in DataNova Corp:

```
SELECT * FROM Departments;
```

This command tells the database: "Show me everything in the Departments table."

Learn what's happening:

SELECT => the command to retrieve data ***(Keyword)***

* => all columns ***(Expression)***

FROM => where to get the data ***(Keyword)***

Departments => the name of the table ***(Table Identifier)***

See the output in Figure 1-4.

	DepartmentID	DepartmentName	Manager
1	1	Marketing	Laura Diaz
2	2	Engineering	Sam Patel
3	3	HR	Tina Chen
4	4	Support	Rajiv Nair

Figure 1-4. *Query Output*

Even if you don't have real data yet, understanding this structure is the first step toward thinking in SQL. Although we used "*" notation in the query above, it is never considered a good practice to retrieve all columns from a table. The tables can be huge, and you would be running an expensive operation that might not be useful.

SQL Data Types

Have you noticed the datatype in Figure 1-1?

Now before we end our day, let's learn more about Data Types in SQL and why it is important to learn them.

A SQL data type defines the values a column can hold. It tells the database whether a column should store numbers, text, dates, or other forms of data. Just like a library uses categories to organize books, a database uses data types to organize and manage information.

Why Are Data Types Important?

Choosing the correct data type ensures accuracy, efficiency, and reliability.

Think of a library: every book has a designated section—mystery, history, science, or fiction. Finding what you need would be frustrating and time-consuming if mystery novels were shelved in the cookbook aisle. Data types in SQL work the same way. They ensure numbers, text, and dates are stored in the right "sections," so your queries run smoothly and return correct results.

Data types provide three main benefits:

- **Storage and Performance**: Using an appropriate data type saves disk space and improves query performance.

- **Validation**: Data types prevent invalid data from being stored (e.g., text in a numeric column).

- **Operations**: The data type determines possible operations (e.g., adding numbers, comparing dates, or concatenating text).

The Role of Size in Data Types

Many SQL data types require you to define a size or precision. This specifies how much space a column can use and how exact its values can be. For example:

- VARCHAR(50) can hold up to 50 characters of text.

- DECIMAL(10,2) can store numbers up to 10 digits long with 2 digits after the decimal point.

Choosing the right size is essential. If you allocate too little, you risk data being cut off or rejected. If you allocate too much, you may waste storage and reduce performance.

For example, in Figure 1-1, each column has an assigned data type and size. For example, by defining FirstName as VARCHAR(50), we're instructing SQL to store up to 50 characters for each first name entry—just enough space for most real-world names, while keeping storage efficient.

Common SQL Data Types

Although names vary slightly across SQL systems (MySQL, SQL Server, PostgreSQL, Oracle), most databases support these categories:

- **Numeric Types**: INT, BIGINT, DECIMAL, NUMERIC, FLOAT, DOUBLE—store whole numbers or decimals.

- **Character Types**: CHAR, VARCHAR, TEXT—store fixed or variable length text.

- **Date and Time Types**: DATE, TIME, DATETIME, TIMESTAMP—store temporal values.

- **Boolean Types**: BOOLEAN or BIT—store TRUE or FALSE values.

- **Binary Types**: BLOB, VARBINARY—store images, files, or other binary data.

Key Takeaways
Concepts You Learned Today

- What SQL is and why it's important

- How relational databases are structured

- How to set up a simple SQL environment

- How to write and understand your first SELECT query

Best Practice of the Day

Never write SQL as a one-liner. Use proper formatting for readability. Example:

SELECT FirstName, LastName /* *All SQL Keywords capitalized* */

FROM Employees e /* *FROM in next line* */

JOIN Departments d ON e.DepartmentID = d.DepartmentID

WHERE d.DepartmentName = 'HR'; /* *WHERE in next line* */

Common Mistakes to Avoid

Don't rely on SELECT *. Always select only the columns you need. It improves clarity and performance.

SQL in the Age of AI—Understanding Databases and SQL

In the age of AI, tools can generate SQL for you—but they can't tell if the data model is flawed or if your schema design will scale. What you learned today helps you understand the structure behind the query, so you can ask better questions and build smarter systems.

Coming Up on Monday

You'll learn how to **filter and sort your data** using WHERE, ORDER BY, and logical operators—perfect for answering your first CEO-level questions like "Who earns the most?" or "Who's in Marketing?"

CHAPTER 2

Monday: Querying Data—Retrieving What You Need by Filtering and Sorting

Goal: Kickoff! This week, we will understand how to filter and sort data using SQL's most essential tools: SELECT, WHERE, ORDER BY, and logical operators. This chapter builds a strong foundation in querying real-world datasets with clarity and control.

Monday at DataNova Corp: Starting to Ask Smart Questions

It's your second day as CEO of DataNova Corp, and you're eager to make informed decisions about your team. You need to answer questions like

- Who works in Marketing?

- Who earns more than $80000?

- Which departments have team members in Asia?

© Bhumika Shah and Devtosh Dubey 2026
B. Shah and D. Dubey, *SQL in a Week*, Apress Pocket Guides,
https://doi.org/10.1007/979-8-8688-2102-8_2

To do that, you need to **filter and sort your employee data**, and today, SQL will teach you how.

SELECT: Choosing Specific Columns

So far, we've used SELECT * to grab everything from a table. Let's improve that.

Instead of:

```
SELECT * FROM Employees;
```

Try this:
```
SELECT FirstName, LastName, DepartmentID FROM Employees;
```

See output in Figure 2-1.

	FirstName	LastName	DepartmentID
1	Alice	Johnson	1
2	Bob	Lee	2
3	Carlos	Ramirez	3
4	Diana	Wang	4
5	Ethan	Kim	2
6	Fiona	Davis	1
7	George	Clark	2
8	Hannah	Zhang	3
9	Ivan	Petrov	4
10	Jenny	Nguyen	2

Figure 2-1. *Query Output*

This is clearer, faster, and only gives you what you need. It's best practice to avoid * in professional environments. Please note that the names of columns match exactly as they appear in the database.

WHERE: Filtering Your Results

The WHERE clause lets you set conditions for what data to include. For example:

If you want to know all employees where DepartmentID = 1:

```
SELECT FirstName, LastName
FROM Employees
WHERE DepartmentID = 1;
```

Output is shown in Figure 2-2.

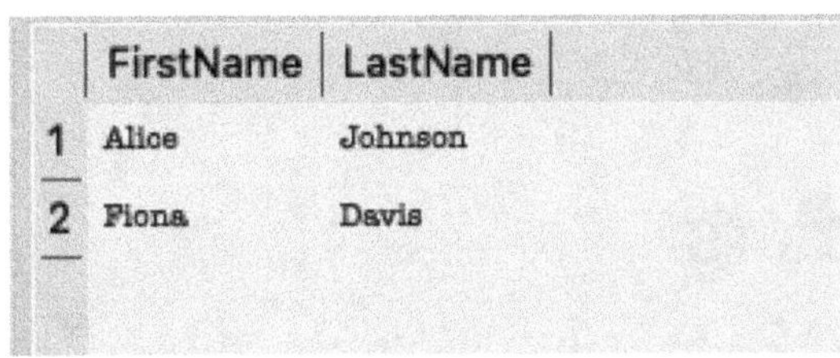

Figure 2-2. *Query Output*

Query Interpretation

- SELECT FirstName, LastName

  This tells the database what columns you want to retrieve. In this case, you're asking for just the FirstName and LastName columns.

- FROM Employees

  This tells SQL where to look—the source table is
  Employees. Think of it like this: "Search inside the
  Employees list."

- WHERE DepartmentID = 1

  This is the filter condition. It only returns rows where
  the DepartmentID column contains the value 1.
  Without this, you'd get names from all departments.

Now that we've learned how to use the three basic SQL commands—
SELECT, FROM, and WHERE—it's time to go a step further. While using
the WHERE clause to filter data, we often need to specify conditions
such as equals, greater than, or less than. This is where **SQL operators**
come into play. Let's explore how these operators help us define precise
conditions within the WHERE clause to make our queries more powerful
and accurate.

SQL Operators

Operators in SQL help you **define conditions** and **compare values**,
making your queries dynamic and powerful. Think of them as the
grammar rules that shape your database conversations.

You can also use operators like

```
= equals
!= not equal
> greater than
< less than
>=, <=
BETWEEN, LIKE, IN, IS NULL
```

Example:

```
Now, you want to have a call with employees making over 80K USD
```

```
SELECT DISTINCT
FirstName,
LastName,
DepartmentID,
Salary
FROM Employees
WHERE
Salary > 80000;
```

See output in Figure 2-3.

	FirstName	LastName	DepartmentID	Salary
1	Bob	Lee	2	95000
2	Ethan	Kim	2	98000
3	George	Clark	2	105000
4	Jenny	Nguyen	2	97000

Figure 2-3. *Query Output*

This week, you only want to meet with employees working at the London and New York locations.

```
SELECT DISTINCT
FirstName,
LastName,
Location
FROM Employees
WHERE Location IN ('New York', 'London');
```

See output in Figure 2-4.

	FirstName	LastName	Location
1	Alice	Johnson	New York
2	Carlos	Ramirez	London

Figure 2-4. *Query Output*

These SQL operators are the backbone of how we interact with data—simple in syntax, yet powerful in their ability to refine results. By mastering them, we can ask precise questions and extract precisely what we need. Whether we filter by salary, location, or job title, these operators help transform a raw table into a meaningful answer. Remember: a well-placed WHERE clause with the right operator can turn an overwhelming dataset into a sharp business insight.

Have you noticed the "AND" operator?

Logical Operators: AND, OR, NOT

Now that you've mastered filtering individual conditions using SQL operators, let's take it further. In real-world scenarios, decisions often depend on **multiple conditions**, and that's where logical operators come in. You can create more powerful queries that mirror complex business logic with AND, OR, and NOT.

Now, you can combine conditions:

Select Employees where DepartmentID = 1 and have a Salary greater than 60K

```
SELECT
FirstName,
```

```
LastName,
DepartmentID,
Location
FROM Employees
WHERE
    DepartmentID = 1
    AND Salary > 60000;
```

See output in Figure 2-5.

	FirstName	LastName	DepartmentID	Location
1	Alice	Johnson	1	New York
2	Fiona	Davis	1	New York

Figure 2-5. *Query Output*

Example of "OR":

```
Select Employees at Seoul and Bangalore locations
SELECT
    FirstName,
    LastName,
    DepartmentID,
    Location
FROM Employees
WHERE
Location = 'Seoul' OR Location = 'Bangalore';
```

See output in Figure 2-6.

	FirstName	LastName	DepartmentID	Location
1	Diana	Wang	4	Bangalore
2	Ethan	Kim	2	Seoul
3	Ivan	Petrov	4	Bangalore

Figure 2-6. *Query Output*

Example of "NOT":

```
Select all employees except where DepartmentID = 1
SELECT
    FirstName,
    LastName,
    DepartmentID
FROM Employees
WHERE
    NOT DepartmentID = 1;
```

See output in Figure 2-7.

	FirstName	LastName	DepartmentID
1	Bob	Lee	2
2	Carlos	Ramirez	3
3	Diana	Wang	4
4	Ethan	Kim	2
5	George	Clark	2
6	Hannah	Zhang	3
7	Ivan	Petrov	4
8	Jenny	Nguyen	2

Figure 2-7. *Query Output*

Hence, Logical combinations allow complex filtering based on business rules. These operators—LIKE, AND, OR, and NOT—help you ask more nuanced questions by combining multiple conditions. Once you've filtered the right data, the next step is to **sort it**—and that's where the ORDER BY clause comes in.

Let's summarize all SQL Operators.

Comparison Operators

These allow you to compare column values (Table 2-1).

Table 2-1. *Comparing column values*

Operator	Meaning	Example
=	Equals	`Salary = 80000`
!= or <>	Not equal	`Department != 'HR'`
>	Greater than	`Salary > 50000`
<	Less than	`Age < 40`
>=	Greater than or equal	`Experience >= 5`
<=	Less than or equal	`JoiningDate <= '2023-01-01'`

Logical Operators

Use these to combine multiple conditions (Table 2-2).

Table 2-2. *Combining multiple conditions*

Operator	Use Case	Example
AND	Both conditions must be true	`DepartmentName = 'HR' AND Salary > 60000`
OR	At least one condition must be true	`Location = 'Tokyo' OR Location = 'Bangalore'`
NOT	Negates the condition	`NOT DepartmentName = 'Support'`

Special Operators

SQL has a few clever helpers that simplify your life (Table 2-3).

Table 2-3. *Ways to simplify*

Operator	Purpose	Example
IN	Check multiple values	`Location IN ('New York', 'London')`
BETWEEN	Check range	`Salary BETWEEN 60000 AND 90000`
LIKE	Pattern matching with wildcards	`FirstName LIKE 'A%'`
IS NULL	Check for missing values	`Email IS NULL`

ORDER BY: Sorting Your Data

Use ORDER BY to sort results:

```
You want to analyze employees' salaries (who were paid the
highest, huh?):
```

```
SELECT
    FirstName,
    Salary
FROM Employees
ORDER BY Salary DESC;
```

See output in Figure 2-8.

	FirstName	Salary
1	Ethan	98000
2	Bob	95000
3	Alice	72000
4	Carlos	65000
5	Diana	60000

Figure 2-8. *Query Output*

```
ASC = Ascending (default)
DESC = Descending
```

You can sort by multiple columns:

```
Also, check employee salary by Location
SELECT
FirstName,
Salary,
Location
FROM Employees
ORDER BY Location ASC, Salary DESC;
```

See output in Figure 2-9.

	FirstName	Salary	Location
1	Diana	60000	Bangalore
2	Ivan	59000	Bangalore
3	Hannah	67000	London
4	Carlos	65000	London
5	Alice	72000	New York
6	Fiona	71000	New York
7	George	105000	San Francisco
8	Bob	95000	San Francisco
9	Ethan	98000	Seoul
10	Jenny	97000	Tokyo

Figure 2-9. *Query Output*

From WHERE filters to logical operators and ORDER BY, you've now seen how SQL statements work together to ask smart, structured questions. These building blocks are the start of writing clean, purposeful queries that drive real decisions.

Before we wrap up Monday, there's one small habit that makes a big difference—**writing comments**. Whether you're working alone or as part of a team, adding comments to your SQL queries helps explain your logic, making your code easier to understand, maintain, and debug. Let's look at how to do it right.

How to Write Comments in SQL

In SQL, comments help explain your code, and they are **not executed** by the database.

There are two ways to write comments:

1. **Single-Line Comment**

   Use two dashes -- for a one-line comment.

   ```
   -- This query fetches employees in the Marketing
   department
   ```
   a.   `SELECT * FROM Employees WHERE DepartmentID = 3;`

2. **Multi-Line Comment**

   Use /**/ to write longer or multi-line comments.

   ```
   /*
     This query returns all employee details
     for those working in the Marketing department.
   */
   SELECT * FROM Employees WHERE DepartmentID = 3;
   ```

Use comments to document your logic, explain joins, or leave notes for your future self or team!

Key Takeaways

Concepts You Learned Today

- Selecting specific columns instead of using *

- Filtering rows with WHERE and logical operators

- Sorting results with ORDER BY and understanding sort direction

- Combining multiple conditions using AND, OR, NOT

Good Coding Practice: Use comments to document the logic behind your code, making it easier to understand and maintain later.

Best Practice of the Day

Always **specify the columns** you need, especially in production systems. It improves query performance and readability.

Use filters to restrict the data you need, and comments to explain the story behind your code.

Common Mistakes to Avoid

Don't forget quotes around strings in conditions. For example, WHERE DepartmentName = Marketing will fail. Correct it as

```
WHERE DepartmentName = 'Marketing'
```

SQL in the Age of AI—SELECT, WHERE, ORDER BY

AI can generate a SELECT query in seconds, but that doesn't guarantee correct results. For example, you might pull thousands of irrelevant rows if the WHERE filter is missing. If the ORDER BY clause is wrong, the data could appear confusing, hiding the insights you need. Therefore, understanding these commands matters more than ever in the age of AI. Think of AI as an assistant that drafts your query, but **you** are the editor. Your skill with SELECT, WHERE, and ORDER BY allows you to check whether the AI's query is accurate, refine its logic, and ensure the output honestly answers your business question.

In short, AI can save you time, but your SQL knowledge ensures the results are trustworthy

Coming Up on Tuesday

You'll learn how to **join multiple tables** to unlock even more value from your data—one of the most powerful concepts in SQL!

CHAPTER 3

Tuesday: Joins— Connecting the Tables

Goal: Understand how to retrieve and combine data from multiple tables using JOIN operations, a key skill for handling real-world relational databases. In real-world systems, information is intentionally spread across multiple tables based on their relationships (cardinality)—such as one-to-many or many-to-many. JOINs allow you to bring that related information together in one place. By learning how to use JOINs, you'll be able to connect data such as employees to their departments, departments to their projects, and employees to the projects they work on. These relationships are common in business environments and understanding them is essential for working confidently with relational databases.

Tuesday at DataNova Corp: Seeing the Full Picture

It's Tuesday at DataNova Corp, and you're starting to realize that one table can only tell part of the story.

© Bhumika Shah and Devtosh Dubey 2026
B. Shah and D. Dubey, *SQL in a Week*, Apress Pocket Guides,
https://doi.org/10.1007/979-8-8688-2102-8_3

You know the names, locations, and departments of your employees, but now you want to understand

- Which Department does each employee belong to

- Who their team leads are

- How department performance is measured

To get these answers, you need to **combine data from multiple related tables.** Today, you'll learn how to use **JOINs** to connect those dots.

Why Do We Store Data in Different Tables?

- **Speed and Efficiency**: If we put everything in one massive table, it would slow down our queries and take longer to load. Smaller, focused tables are much faster to work with.

- **Better Organization**: Keeping related data in separate tables (like Employees, Departments, Projects) makes everything easier to manage and understand, just like organizing your files into folders.

- **Logical Separation**: You wouldn't keep summer and winter clothes in the same closet, right? Same with data. Splitting it up helps avoid confusion and keeps things tidy.

- **Scalability**: Well-structured tables can grow independently. This is helpful when some types of data grow faster than others.

- **Best Practices**: In data engineering, we often use something called a **Star Schema** to organize tables around a central "fact" table—look it up if you're curious!

Before We Join Tables: Understanding Table Relationships

Before we start combining tables using JOINs, it's useful to understand how tables can relate to each other in a database. These relationships are referred to as **cardinality**, and they describe how many records in one table can be associated with records in another table. Understanding cardinality will give you a stronger intuition for how JOINs behave and why certain query results look the way they do.

In our company database, we are working with four main tables:

- Departments

- Employees

- Projects

- Assignments

Let's see how they relate to each other.

Relationships in Our Data Model

Table 3-1 shows relationships and their meaning and interpretation.

Table 3-1. *Relationships*

Relationship Type	Tables Involved	What It Means in Our Data	Business Interpretation
One-to-Many (1:N)	Departments → Employees	Each department can have many employees, but each employee belongs to only one department (via DepartmentID).	One department, many employees. For example, Engineering may have several employees.
One-to-Many (1:N)	Departments → Projects	Each department can own many projects, but each project is owned by exactly one department (via DepartmentID).	One department, many projects. For example, Marketing may handle multiple campaigns.
Many-to-Many (M:N)	Employees ↔ Projects (through Assignments)	An employee can work on multiple projects, and a project can have multiple employees. The Assignments table links them using EmployeeID and ProjectID.	One employee on many projects, and one project with many employees. For example, Bob can work on both "AI Chatbot" and "Cloud Migration," along with other team members.

Why These Relationships Matter for JOINs

When you write JOINs, you are basically asking the database to **follow these relationships** and bring back combined information.

- When you join Departments and Employees, you are working with a **One-to-Many** relationship.

  One row from Departments can match many rows from Employees. So, the department row is repeated for each employee in that department. This is expected and correct.

- When you join Departments and Projects, it's again **One-to-Many**.

  One department may appear on multiple rows—one for each project it owns.

- When you join Employees and Projects through Assignments, you are working with a **Many-to-Many** relationship.

  Each combination of an employee and a project they are assigned to becomes a separate row. This is why, in reports, you might see the same employee name repeated across multiple projects, and the same project name repeated across multiple employees.

Understanding these relationships upfront will make JOINs much easier to read and interpret. Instead of being surprised by "duplicate-looking rows," you will understand that

- **One-to-Many** relationships naturally create multiple rows per "parent" record.

- **Many-to-Many** relationships often involve a bridge table (like Assignments) and can produce even more combinations.

With this foundation in place, we're now ready to start writing JOINs using our Employees, Departments, Projects, and Assignments tables (Figure 3-1).

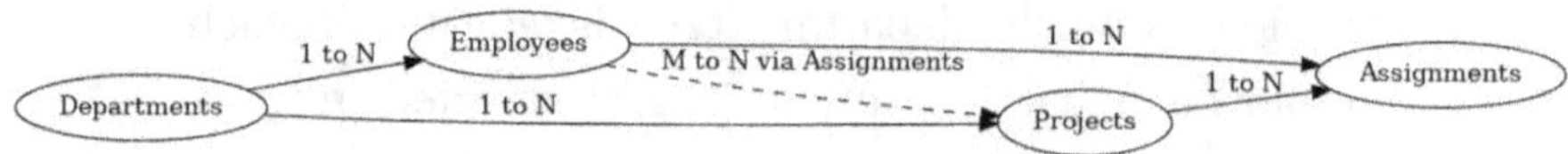

Figure 3-1. *Writing JOINs*

JOINs: Understanding Relationships Between Tables

In relational databases, data is normalized and split into multiple tables. For example:

Employees Table:

- EmployeeID

- FirstName

- LastName

- DepartmentID

Departments Table:

- DepartmentID

- DepartmentName

- ManagerID

The two tables are connected by a common key: DepartmentID. We can use this key to pull related information together. Let's also quickly talk about syntax:

1. You always have the primary table in the From clause, followed by the table that you are joining.

2. It's best practice to use aliases when joining multiple
    tables because they make your queries easier to read
    and help the database clearly understand which
    table each column belongs to, especially when
    different tables have columns with the same name.

```
SYNTAX:
FROM <MAIN TABLE> as <ALIAS1>
<JOIN (INNER, LEFT, RIGHT)> as <ALIAS2> ON <ALIAS1>.<COL_NAME>
= <ALIAS2>.<COL_NAME>
FROM main_table a
LEFT JOIN secondary_table  as b ON a.commonkey = b.commonkey

*The "as" keyword is not mandatory. I would highly recommend
using it as it keeps the code clean, readable, and organized.
```

INNER JOIN: Matching Records in Both Tables

```
SELECT
a.DepartmentName,
a.Manager,
p.ProjectName,
p.Budget
FROM Departments a
INNER JOIN Projects p on a.DepartmentID = p.DepartmentID;
```

See output in Figure 3-2.

	DepartmentName	Manager	ProjectName	Budget
1	Marketing	Laura Diaz	Brand Redesign	150000
2	Engineering	Sam Patel	AI Chatbot	300000
3	HR	Tina Chen	Recruitment Drive	80000
4	Support	Rajiv Nair	Helpdesk Upgrade	60000
5	Marketing	Laura Diaz	Product Launch	200000
6	Engineering	Sam Patel	Cloud Migration	400000
7	HR	Tina Chen	Employee Onboarding	95000
8	Support	Rajiv Nair	Ticket System Revamp	75000

Figure 3-2. *Query Output*

This will give you a list of Department Name, Manager, Project Name, and Budget.

- INNER JOIN returns only the rows that match in both tables, you can use these to map ID to their corresponding names. Like we did above.

- Since the output of INNER JOIN returns matched rows from both tables, it is important to keep in mind that if left table has 100 rows and right table has 200 rows but only 5 of them overlap, the result set will have these 5 rows.

- Aliases (a and p) make your queries shorter and easier to read and also you can leverage autocomplete features offered by most sql editors.

LEFT JOIN: Keeping All Records from the Left Table

Sometimes you want to see all employees, even if their department data is missing.

```
SELECT
    e.FirstName,
    e.LastName,
    d.DepartmentName
FROM Employees e
LEFT JOIN Departments d ON e.DepartmentID = d.DepartmentID;
```

See output in Figure 3-3.

	FirstName	LastName	DepartmentName
1	Alice	Johnson	Marketing
2	Bob	Lee	Engineering
3	Carlos	Ramirez	HR
4	Diana	Wang	Support
5	Ethan	Kim	Engineering
6	Fiona	Davis	Marketing
7	George	Clark	Engineering
8	Hannah	Zhang	HR
9	Ivan	Petrov	Support
10	Jenny	Nguyen	Engineering

Figure 3-3. *Query Output*

- LEFT JOIN includes all employees, even if they don't have a matching department.

- Non-matching department fields will show as NULL.

RIGHT JOIN and FULL OUTER JOIN

- **RIGHT JOIN**: Returns all records from the right table and matched records from the left. It will include all departments, even if there is no employee in the Department

- **FULL OUTER JOIN**: Returns all records when there is a match in either table. It will include all employees and departments (including employees without a department and departments without employees).

  Cool! Right? However, an outer join is the most expensive join; therefore, it is not advisable to use it unless needed.

Note   Not all database systems support FULL OUTER JOIN (e.g., MySQL requires a workaround).

Joining More Than Two Tables

You can join as many tables as needed. For example, if you had a "Manager" table

You want to check each employee's departments and the department's managers.

```
SELECT e.FirstName, d.DepartmentName, m.ManagerName
FROM Employees e
JOIN Departments d ON e.DepartmentID = d.DepartmentID
JOIN Managers m ON d.ManagerID = m.ManagerID;
```

This query brings everything together showing each employee alongside their department and the manager of that department. By using joins, you're essentially connecting related pieces of information from different tables into one clear result, just like linking chapters of a story to see the bigger picture.

Now that we've explored different types of SQL joins—such as INNER JOIN, LEFT JOIN, RIGHT JOIN, and FULL OUTER JOIN—you can see how powerful they are in combining data across multiple tables. Joins are essential for building meaningful relationships between datasets and answering complex business questions. However, as your data grows, how you write joins can significantly impact query performance. In the next section, we'll dive into how to optimize joins for efficiency, avoid performance pitfalls, and write queries that scale well with large datasets.

Joins and Their Performance

Let's summarize joins and their performance:

1—INNER JOIN

What It Does: Returns only matching rows from both tables.

Performance: Fastest among joins, since it skips non-matching data.

Best For: Filtering and combining related data (e.g., employees with matching departments).

2-LEFT JOIN (or LEFT OUTER JOIN)

What It Does: Returns all rows from the left table and matched rows from the right table. If no match, it fills in NULLs.

Performance: Slower than INNER JOIN because it has to return unmatched rows too from the left table.

Best For: When you want to keep all data from the primary table (e.g., show all customers, even those with no orders).

3—RIGHT JOIN

What It Does: Opposite of LEFT JOIN. Returns all rows from the right table and matched rows from the left.

Performance: Similar to LEFT JOIN.

Best For: Less commonly used—can often be rewritten as LEFT JOIN by reversing table order.

4—FULL OUTER JOIN

What It Does: Returns all rows from both tables, with NULLs where there is no match.

Performance: Slowest join, as it must combine everything, including unmatched rows from both sides.

Best For: Finding unmatched records from either table (e.g., auditing or syncing records).

5—CROSS JOIN

What It Does: Returns every combination of rows (Cartesian product).

Performance: Very slow and heavy if not limited— can explode in size!

Best For: Rare cases like generating test data or combinations.

Performance Tips: Making Your Queries CEO-Level Efficient

As the CEO of DataNova Corp, speed matters—whether it's team performance or query execution. Here's how to make your SQL queries run smoother and smarter:

- **Always Index the Columns Used in Joins:**

  Indexes are like fast-access directories. If you're joining tables on EmployeeID, make sure it's indexed. Otherwise, SQL has to scan the whole table—costly when your company scales.

- **Avoid SELECT *:**

  Pulling all columns clutters your result and slows performance. Instead, be specific—like SELECT e.FirstName, e.LastName, d.DepartmentName—and use aliases (e, d) to clarify which column belongs to which table.

- **Avoid joining large tables unnecessarily:**

  Every join has a cost. Think like a CEO reviewing only relevant reports—only join what you need to answer your business question.

- **Use INNER JOIN > OUTER JOIN when logic allows:**

  INNER JOIN is leaner and faster. Use OUTER JOIN only when you truly need to include unmatched rows. The lighter your join, the quicker the insights.

Just like a CEO cares about performance and efficiency in every corner of the business, **SQL performance matters too**. Writing queries that are not only correct but also optimized can make a big difference—especially when working with large datasets or time-sensitive decisions.

Key Takeaways

Concepts You Learned Today

- How relational data is structured across multiple tables

- Using INNER JOIN to combine records with matching keys

- Using LEFT JOIN to retain unmatched records from one side

- How to join more than two tables

Best Practice of the Day

Use table aliases (e, d, etc.) to simplify queries and improve readability, especially in JOINs.

Common Mistakes to Avoid

Forgetting the ON condition in a JOIN can lead to a Cartesian product—a huge, meaningless dataset.

SQL in the Age of AI—JOINs

AI can suggest joins, but it won't always know your data relationships. Understanding joins lets you **verify and tweak AI-generated queries**, especially when working across complex, relational tables.

Coming Up on Wednesday

You'll learn how to **group and summarize** your data using GROUP BY, HAVING, and SQL aggregate functions to generate team insights and analytics.

CHAPTER 4

Wednesday: Aggregations— Making Sense of the Numbers

Goal: Help you learn how to summarize and analyze data using SQL aggregation functions and GROUP BY, bringing clarity to patterns and trends in their data.

Wednesday at DataNova Corp: Discovering Insights from Data

Happy Wednesday, CEO! You're halfway through your SQL journey, and it's time to take things up a notch. You've connected your tables, met your team, and now you want to ask bigger questions like

- What's the average salary for each Department?

- How many employees are in each location?

- Which departments have the highest headcount?

© Bhumika Shah and Devtosh Dubey 2026
B. Shah and D. Dubey, *SQL in a Week*, Apress Pocket Guides,
https://doi.org/10.1007/979-8-8688-2102-8_4

These aren't just data points—they're insights that can drive real decisions. Today, you'll learn how to **group, count, and calculate** with SQL to become a truly data-driven leader.

Let's dive in with confidence and curiosity!

Aggregation Functions: Your Analytical Toolbox

Aggregate functions in SQL are used to perform calculations on multiple rows of data and return a single summary value.

Why do we need Aggregate functions?

> **Raw data isn't always meaningful**—tables with hundreds or thousands of rows don't provide insights unless we summarize them.

> **No one wants to manually scan through 100+ rows** just to find out simple answers like average salary, total revenue, or highest expense.

SQL provides powerful functions to perform calculations across groups of data:

- **COUNT()**: Counts the argument passed to function

- **SUM()**: Adds up values

- **AVG()**: Calculates the average

- **MIN()/MAX()**: Finds the smallest or largest value

Example:

```
#You want to know the number of employees in each Department.
SELECT
    d.DepartmentName,
```

```
COUNT (*) AS Row_Count,
    COUNT(EmployeeID) as counts_of_Employees
FROM
    Employees e
JOIN Departments d on d.DepartmentID = e.DepartmentID
GROUP BY 1;
```

Syntax Breakdown:

1. **SELECT DepartmentID, COUNT (*) AS EmployeeCount**

    - This tells SQL to return two columns:

        - **DepartmentName** (the group identifier).

        - COUNT (*) counts the number of employees **in each Department**(similar to counting rows for each Department Name).

        - On the other hand if you did count(distinct EmployeeID) will give you counts of distinct Employee ID for each department.

        - AS EmployeeCount gives a user-friendly name (alias) to the count column.

2. **FROM Employees**

    - This specifies the **table** FROM which the data is coming—Employees in this case.

3. **JOIN Departments**

    - You join Departments table with Employees table in order to get the Department Name.

    - You could have just used the DepartmentId but in this case, we decided to pull in the Department Name as well.

4. **GROUP BY DepartmentName**

- This groups all the rows that have the **same DepartmentName** together.

- Then the COUNT (*) is calculated **within each group**.

This may give you duplicate records, for example, Alice and her Department may be written twice in the database. (Strange? But real-world databases are not always clean)

Now try this:

```
SELECT DepartmentID, COUNT (Distinct EmployeeId) AS EmployeeCount
FROM Employees
GROUP BY DepartmentID;
```

This query will count Alice only once because we're using DISTINCT, and replacing * with the specific Employee column name improves performance efficiency.

GROUP BY: Organizing Your Data

The GROUP BY clause lets you group rows that share the same value in one or more columns:

```
# You want to know how much salary is being paid for each
location? Is the budget for the New York office greater than
that for London? Let's find out.
SELECT Location, AVG(Salary) AS AvgSalary
FROM Employees
GROUP BY Location;
```

You can group by any column(s) to see patterns and breakdowns (Figure 4-1).

	Location	AvgSalary
1	Bangalore	59500.0
2	London	66000.0
3	New York	71500.0
4	San Francisco	100000.0
5	Seoul	98000.0
6	Tokyo	97000.0

Figure 4-1. *Query Output*

HAVING: Filtering Grouped Results

HAVING works like WHERE, but for aggregated results.

```
#You want to know the departments with more than three
employees.
SELECT DepartmentID, COUNT(*) AS EmployeeCount
FROM Employees
GROUP BY DepartmentID
HAVING COUNT(*) > 3;
```

See output in Figure 4-2.

	DepartmentID	EmployeeCount
1	2	4

Figure 4-2. *Query Output*

WHERE Vs. HAVING

WHERE filters rows before aggregation; HAVING filters groups after aggregation.

#Now you want to find all departments that have employees earning **more than $70000**, and you want to see **only those departments** where the **average salary is above $80000**.

Let's break that into two filters:

Use WHERE to filter **individual rows**

Use HAVING to filter **aggregated results**

```
SELECT DepartmentID, AVG(Salary) AS AvgSalary
FROM Employees
WHERE Salary > 70000
GROUP BY DepartmentID
HAVING AVG(Salary) > 80000;
```

Explanation:

- **WHERE Salary > 70000**: Filters out rows before aggregation

- **GROUP BY DepartmentID**: Groups the remaining records by DepartmentID

- **HAVING AVG(Salary) > 80000**: Filters the grouped results after calculating the average

Think about this if you want to find Departments with average salary greater than 100000 and employee location is New York.

In this case:

1. New York Filter goes in the WHERE clause.

2. Average Salary filter should be applied after you have calculated the Departments Average Salary.

Key Takeaways

Concepts You Learned Today

- How to use COUNT(), AVG(), SUM(), MIN(), and MAX()

- Grouping data with GROUP BY to create summaries

- Filtering group results using HAVING

- Combining JOIN with GROUP BY for powerful breakdowns

Best Practice of the Day

Use clear aliases like TotalEmployees or AvgSalary to make your result sets easier to read and understand.

Common Mistakes to Avoid

Don't use WHERE to filter grouped results—that's what HAVING is for!

SQL in the Age of AI—GROUP BY

AI may write a GROUP BY, but it doesn't always understand your business logic. With today's knowledge, you'll catch incorrect aggregations, misused columns, or summaries that don't tell the real story.

Coming Up on Thursday

Now that you know how to retrieve, join, and analyze data, it's time to take your SQL skills to the next level. Tomorrow, we will explore subqueries, Common Table Expressions (CTEs), and built-in SQL functions. These tools will help you break complex problems into smaller steps and write cleaner, more powerful queries that reflect real-world data challenges.

CHAPTER 5

Thursday: Subqueries and CTEs—Thinking in Layers

Goal: Help you write modular, readable SQL by introducing **subqueries**, **Common Table Expressions (CTEs) and Functions**, allowing for better structure and more powerful logic in their queries.

Thursday at DataNova Corp: Smarter Queries for a Smarter CEO

Welcome to Thursday, CEO! You're doing an incredible job digging into your company's data. Today, we level up your skills by learning how to **think in layers**. Sometimes you need to answer questions that are too complex for one flat query:

- Who earns more than the average salary in their department?

- What are the top three highest-paying roles per department?

- Can we simplify a long query into logical, readable chunks?

© Bhumika Shah and Devtosh Dubey 2026
B. Shah and D. Dubey, *SQL in a Week*, Apress Pocket Guides,
https://doi.org/10.1007/979-8-8688-2102-8_5

These are the types of questions where **subqueries** and **CTEs** shine. Let's learn how to write smarter, clearer SQL that's easier to understand, debug, and scale.

Subqueries: Queries Within Queries

A subquery is a SQL query nested inside another query. It helps break down complex logic step-by-step.

Example:

```
SELECT FirstName, Salary
 FROM Employees
 WHERE Salary > (
   SELECT AVG(Salary)
   FROM Employees
);
```

See output in Figure 5-1.

	FirstName	Salary
1	Bob	95000
2	Ethan	98000
3	George	105000
4	Jenny	97000

Figure 5-1. *Query Output*

This returns all employees who earn more than the **average salary**.

Correlated Subqueries

These are subqueries that reference a column from the outer query:

```
SELECT e.FirstName, e.Salary
 FROM Employees e
 WHERE e.Salary > (
   SELECT AVG(Salary)
   FROM Employees
   WHERE DepartmentID = e.DepartmentID
);
```

See output in Figure 5-2.

	FirstName	Salary
1	Alice	72000
2	Diana	60000
3	George	105000
4	Hannah	67000

Figure 5-2. *Query Output*

Now you're comparing employees to the **average within their department**.

Common Table Expressions (CTEs): Clean and Modular

A CTE makes your query more readable by defining temporary result sets that can be referenced later:

```sql
WITH DepartmentAverages AS (
    SELECT DepartmentID, AVG(Salary) AS AvgSalary
    FROM Employees
    GROUP BY DepartmentID
)
SELECT e.FirstName, e.Salary, d.AvgSalary
FROM Employees e
JOIN DepartmentAverages d
  ON e.DepartmentID = d.DepartmentID
WHERE e.Salary > d.AvgSalary;
```

See output in Figure 5-3.

	FirstName	Salary	AvgSalary
1	Alice	72000	71800.0
2	Diana	60000	59800.0
3	George	105000	98780.0
4	Hannah	67000	66000.0

Figure 5-3. *Query Output*

This does the same as above, but **in a cleaner way**. CTEs are easier to debug and extend.

SQL Functions: Reuse and Simplify Logic

SQL has two kinds of functions:

1. **Built-in functions** like LEN(), ROUND(), GETDATE(), LOWER(), UPPER(), and ISNULL().

2. **User-defined functions (UDFs)**—custom logic that can be reused.

Example: Find names in lowercase for analytics normalization.

```
SELECT LOWER(FirstName) AS LowercaseName FROM Employees;
```

Want to create your own function? You can:

```
CREATE FUNCTION dbo.GetAnnualSalary (@monthly DECIMAL(10,2))
RETURNS DECIMAL(10,2)ASBEGIN    RETURN @monthly * 12END;
```

Now use it like this:

```
SELECT FirstName, dbo.GetAnnualSalary(Salary) AS AnnualSal FROM
Employees;
```

Note   SQL Server Syntax Only

This example uses T-SQL (SQL Server) syntax and is for conceptual illustration only — it will not run in SQLite or other databases as-is. Each database platform handles user-defined functions differently. Consult your database's official documentation for the correct syntax.

Here are some most common functions (Table 5-1).

Table 5-1. *Common SQL functions*

Function Name	Description / Use Case Example
LEN()	Returns length of a string → LEN(FirstName)
LOWER()	Converts to lowercase → LOWER(FirstName)
UPPER()	Converts to uppercase → UPPER(City)
LEFT(str, n)	Returns first *n* characters → LEFT(Name, 3)
RIGHT(str, n)	Returns last *n* characters → RIGHT(Code, 2)
LTRIM()/RTRIM()	Removes leading/trailing spaces → LTRIM(ProductName)
CHARINDEX()	Finds position of a substring → CHARINDEX('a', Email)
SUBSTRING()	Extracts part of a string → SUBSTRING(Phone, 1, 3)
REPLACE()	Replaces part of string → REPLACE(Name, 'Mr.', '')
CONCAT()	Joins multiple strings → CONCAT(FirstName, ' ', LastName)

Let's combine what you've learned.

Use a subquery inside a WHERE to filter employees who earn more than the max salary in Support department:

```
SELECT * FROM Employees WHERE Salary > ( SELECT MAX(Salary)
FROM Employees WHERE DepartmentID = 4);
```

Use a CTE for reusable sales data(Assuming you have a SalesData table):

```
WITH HighSales AS ( SELECT EmployeeID, Sales FROM
SalesData WHERE Sales > 100000)SELECT e.FirstName,
s.Sales FROM Employees e JOIN HighSales s ON e.EmployeeID =
s.EmployeeID;
```

Note   SalesData is a hypothetical table used here for illustration. In your DataNova Corp database, you could apply this same CTE pattern to the Projects or Assignments tables.

When to Use Subqueries vs. CTEs

CTEs really shine in scenarios where

- **The logic is multi-step.**

  Nobody enjoys scrolling through endless nested subqueries. CTEs give your query structure, breathing room, and clarity.

- **The query is long or reused.**

  If you find yourself referencing the same calculation or expression multiple times, calculate it once in a CTE and reuse it cleanly.

- **You want to debug or validate step-by-step.**

  With CTEs, you can isolate each logical step. For example, you could run SELECT * FROM HighSales to validate that portion before moving on. This makes troubleshooting much easier.

Subqueries are perfectly fine when

- **The logic is small and localized.**

  If the calculation is used once and is simple enough to understand inline, a subquery is more than sufficient.

- **It doesn't need to be referenced again.**

  For one-time filters, expressions, or small lookups, subqueries keep things concise.

- **Readability remains intact.**

  When a subquery doesn't make the code harder to read, there's no need to introduce a CTE.

See Table 5-2 for CTE vs. subqueries.

Table 5-2. *CTE vs. subqueries*

Criteria	CTE (Common Table Expression)	Subquery
Best Use Case	Multi-step, reusable, or complex logic	Small, localized, one-time logic
Readability	High: breaks logic into clear steps	Good only when logic stays short
Reusability	Can be referenced multiple times	Cannot be reused; evaluated inline
Debugging	Easy: each CTE block can be inspected individually	Hard: must trace inside nested expressions
Query Length Fit	Ideal for long or layered queries	Ideal for short and simple queries
Maintenance	Easier to maintain and modify	More difficult when nesting grows
Performance Perspective	Computed once and reused	Computed each time it appears (unless optimized)
Typical Usage	Data transformations, staging, multiple filters, complex joins	Filters, small lookups, quick calculations
Code Structure	Top-down, step-based, readable	Inline and embedded within the main query
Good Example Scenario	Reporting logic, BI transformations, analytical pipelines	Filter by latest date or simple aggregation

Window Functions: Advanced Yet Elegant

Window functions allow you to perform calculations across a set of rows **related to the current row**, without collapsing results like GROUP BY does.

They shine in tasks like

- Ranking employees within departments

- Calculating running totals

- Comparing values across rows

ROW_NUMBER(): Ranking Within Groups

```
SELECT FirstName, DepartmentID,
       ROW_NUMBER() OVER (PARTITION BY DepartmentID ORDER BY
       Salary DESC) AS RankInDept
FROM Employees;
```

See output in Figure 5-4.

	FirstName	DepartmentID	RankInDept
1	Alice	1	1
2	Fiona	1	2
3	George	2	1
4	Ethan	2	2
5	Jenny	2	3
6	Bob	2	4
7	Hannah	3	1
8	Carlos	3	2
9	Diana	4	1
10	Ivan	4	2

Figure 5-4. *Query Output*

This ranks employees **within each department** by salary.

RANK() and DENSE_RANK()

These functions are similar to ROW_NUMBER() but handle ties differently:

- RANK() skips numbers for ties

- DENSE_RANK() does not

SUM() OVER(): Running Totals and More

```
SELECT FirstName, DepartmentID, Salary,
       SUM(Salary) OVER (PARTITION BY DepartmentID ORDER BY
       Salary) AS DeptRunningTotal
FROM Employees;
```

See output in Figure 5-5.

	FirstName	DepartmentID	Salary	DeptRunningTotal
1	Fiona	1	71000	71000
2	Alice	1	72000	143000
3	Bob	2	95000	95000
4	Jenny	2	97000	192000
5	Ethan	2	98000	290000
6	George	2	105000	395000
7	Carlos	3	65000	65000
8	Hannah	3	67000	132000
9	Ivan	4	59000	59000
10	Diana	4	60000	119000

Figure 5-5. *Query Output*

This calculates a **cumulative salary total** for each department.
Lead Window Function:

As a CEO, you want to understand across our active projects, are workloads evenly distributed among team members?"

For each project, you want to understand how work is spread from the most heavily loaded person to others, so we can identify potential overload or underutilization.

```
SELECT
    a.ProjectID,
    p.ProjectName,
    a.EmployeeID,
    a.Role,
    a.HoursPerWeek,

    LAG(a.HoursPerWeek) OVER (
        PARTITION BY a.ProjectID
        ORDER BY a.HoursPerWeek DESC
    ) AS PreviousEmployeeHours,

    a.HoursPerWeek
      - LAG(a.HoursPerWeek) OVER (
            PARTITION BY a.ProjectID
            ORDER BY a.HoursPerWeek DESC
        ) AS WorkloadGap

FROM Assignments a
JOIN Projects p
  ON a.ProjectID = p.ProjectID
ORDER BY a.ProjectID, a.HoursPerWeek DESC;
```

See output in Figure 5-6.

	ProjectID	ProjectName	EmployeeID	Role	HoursPerWeek	PreviousEmployeeHours	WorkloadGap
1	101	Brand Redesign	1	Coordinator	10	NULL	NULL
2	102	AI Chatbot	5	AI Engineer	30	NULL	NULL
3	102	AI Chatbot	2	Developer	20	30	-10
4	103	Recruitment Drive	3	HR Lead	18	NULL	NULL
5	104	Helpdesk Upgrade	4	Support Agent	25	NULL	NULL
6	105	Product Launch	6	Marketing Analyst	12	NULL	NULL
7	105	Product Launch	1	Content Creator	10	12	-2
8	106	Cloud Migration	10	DevOps Engineer	28	NULL	NULL
9	106	Cloud Migration	7	Cloud Architect	25	28	-3
10	106	Cloud Migration	2	Lead Engineer	18	25	-10
11	107	Employee Onboarding	8	Trainer	18	NULL	NULL
12	108	Ticket System Revamp	9	IT Support	20	NULL	NULL

Figure 5-6. *Query Output*

Let's pick apart the window functions here.

Step 1: Compare people within the same project

PARTITION BY a.ProjectID

This ensures

Employees are compared only to others on the same project

Step 2: Order by Clause, you need order by clause in your window function to order the rows within the partition field as defined by in the partition by clause.

ORDER BY a.HoursPerWeek DESC

This ordering represents a business concept:

Top row = most loaded person

Rows below = people doing progressively less work

This ordering is crucial. Without it, the comparison would be arbitrary.

Step 3: Use LAG to compare each person to the one above them

```
LAG(a.HoursPerWeek)
```

LAG looks backward within each project to fetch the workload of the person just above

Step 4: Quantify the difference

```
a.HoursPerWeek - LAG(a.HoursPerWeek) AS WorkloadGap
```

Now comparing the rows and the difference in values helps you gather insights

0 → evenly distributed work

Small negative number → slight imbalance

Large negative number → significant imbalance

In the screenshot if you look at the data for Cloud Migration you can see that

- One person is carrying the heaviest load (28 hours).

- The next person is close (25 hours).

- The third person is working 10 hours less → clear imbalance.

Why some rows show NULL:

- The top person per project has **no one above them**.

Rank(), Dense_Rank(), and ROW_NUMBER()

In this scenario, you are the CEO looking at employee salaries across different departments. Instead of focusing on individual salary differences, your goal is to understand how compensation is structured across the organization at a higher level.

You are interested in identifying **salary bands or tiers** within each department so you can clearly see who falls into the higher compensation groups for planning and decision-making during the Annual Operating Plan (AOP). This approach helps you analyze pay distribution without getting distracted by small variations in salary amounts.

You might express your intention like this:

"I want to understand how employee pay is structured across departments without focusing on small individual salary differences. Please group employees into pay tiers instead of showing exact salary values."

Additionally, you want visibility into how employees compare within their department:

"Within each department, show me which employees fall into the higher pay tiers and how they are ranked."

Finally, you care about fairness and consistency, especially where multiple employees earn the same salary:

"I also want to see how rankings behave when multiple employees fall into the same pay tier, so we can make fair promotion and pay decisions."

This is a perfect use case for exploring how **ROW_NUMBER**, **RANK**, and **DENSE_RANK** behave when ordering data inside a partition—in this case, a partition defined by department.

By comparing these ranking methods side-by-side, you'll learn how SQL handles ties, how different types of rankings can be used for business decisions, and how pay bands can be created for reporting without revealing exact compensation figures.

```
WITH banded AS (
  SELECT
      e.DepartmentID,
      e.FirstName,
      e.LastName,
      e.Salary,
```

```
        FLOOR(e.Salary / 10000) * 10000 AS SalaryBand
  FROM Employees e
)
SELECT
    DepartmentID,
    FirstName,
    LastName,
    Salary,
    SalaryBand,

    ROW_NUMBER() OVER (
        PARTITION BY DepartmentID
        ORDER BY SalaryBand DESC, Salary DESC
    ) AS RowNum,

    RANK() OVER (
        PARTITION BY DepartmentID
        ORDER BY SalaryBand DESC
    ) AS BandRank,

    DENSE_RANK() OVER (
        PARTITION BY DepartmentID
        ORDER BY SalaryBand DESC
    ) AS DenseBandRank
FROM banded
ORDER BY DepartmentID, SalaryBand DESC, Salary DESC;
```

See output in Figure 5-7.

	DepartmentID	FirstName	LastName	Salary	SalaryBand	RowNum	BandRank	DenseBandRank
1	1	Alice	Johnson	72000	70000	1	1	1
2	1	Fiona	Davis	71000	70000	2	1	1
3	2	George	Clark	105000	100000	1	1	1
4	2	Ethan	Kim	98000	90000	2	2	2
5	2	Jenny	Nguyen	97000	90000	3	2	2
6	2	Bob	Lee	95000	90000	4	2	2
7	3	Hannah	Zhang	67000	60000	1	1	1
8	3	Carlos	Ramirez	65000	60000	2	1	1
9	4	Diana	Wang	60000	60000	1	1	1
10	4	Ivan	Petrov	59000	50000	2	2	2

Figure 5-7. *Query Output*

This example is pretty helpful in understanding row_number, rank, and dense_rank window function.

ROW_NUMBER

Gives a unique sequence (1, 2, 3…) for each employee within the department.

Even if two people share the same SalaryBand, they still get different row numbers.

Example (Department 1):

Alice and Fiona are both in the 70k band, but RowNum is 1 and 2.

RANK

Gives the same rank for ties (same SalaryBand),

but skips numbers after the tie.

Example (Department 1):

Alice and Fiona are tied in the same band → both get BandRank = 1

The next person in a lower band would jump to rank 3 (rank 2 is skipped) if present.

(The screenshot doesn't show the "skipping" because Dept 1 only has those two rows, but that's the rule.)

DENSE_RANK

Also gives the same rank for ties

but does NOT skip numbers after a tie.

Example (Department 2):

Ethan, Jenny, and Bob are all in the 90k band → all get DenseBandRank = 2

The next lower band (if it existed) would become rank 3 (no gaps).

Difference Between ROW_NUMBER(), RANK(), and DENSE_ RANK() is shown in Table 5-3.

Table 5-3. *Difference between ROW_NUMBER(), RANK(), and DENSE_RANK()*

Feature	ROW_NUMBER()	RANK()	DENSE_RANK()
What it does	Assigns a unique sequential number to each row	Assigns ranking with gaps if ties exist	Assigns ranking without gaps even if ties exist
Ties (same values)	No ties—every row gets a new number	Ties get same rank, next rank jumps	Ties get same rank; next rank does **not** jump
Example scenario	Numbering rows for pagination, ordering	Ranking sales but acknowledging ties	Ranking without skipping numbers
Output Example when 2nd and 3rd rows tie	1, 2, 3, 4	1, 2, 2, 4	1, 2, 2, 3
Use Case in Businesses	Displaying top N rows cleanly	Reward systems (e.g., top sellers)	Leaderboards or category rankings
Performance	Similar to ranking functions	Similar	Similar
Uniqueness	Always unique	Not always	Not always

Key Takeaways

Concepts You Learned Today

- Writing subqueries to filter or compare data

- Using correlated subqueries for dynamic comparisons

- Creating modular logic using `WITH` and CTEs

- Choosing when to use subqueries vs. CTEs

- Using `ROW_NUMBER()`, `RANK()`, and `SUM() OVER` for advanced row-wise analysis

Best Practice of the Day

Break long queries into CTEs to keep your SQL organized and readable—future you (and your team) will thank you.

Common Mistake to Avoid

Don't overuse subqueries when a simple JOIN or CTE can be used. Over-nesting can hurt performance and readability of query.

SQL in the Age of AI—AI and Complex Queries

- AI can generate CTEs and subqueries, but only *you* can provide the logic and context.

- Knowing how to structure them makes you the architect, not just the reviewer.

- Use AI to speed up, not skip the thinking.

Coming Up on Friday

You've made it through an intensive Thursday! Tomorrow, we'll slow down and focus on **query optimization tips, indexing strategies, and interview-friendly SQL hacks**—your well-earned **TGIF session!**

You'll learn how to write **optimized, high-performance queries** using indexes and best practices that scale as your company grows!

CHAPTER 6

Friday: Query Optimization—Write Smart, Run Fast

Goal: TGIF, CEO! You've learned the basics—now it's time to go from good to great. This chapter is designed for those with **intermediate SQL experience** who want to master **performance tuning**, understand **advanced query mechanics**, and prepare for **data analytics interviews** at top-tier tech companies. Let's refine your SQL to a level where it speaks for your skills.

Friday at DataNova Corp: Efficiency Mode Activated

You've worked hard all week, CEO—learning joins, aggregations, subqueries, and window functions. Today, we take a breath and focus on something every pro values: **performance**.

Imagine your queries running on a huge database with millions of records. Will they still perform well? Today, you'll learn how to make your SQL **faster, cleaner, and scalable** with smart practices that every data-driven leader should know.

Let's optimize like a boss.

© Bhumika Shah and Devtosh Dubey 2026
B. Shah and D. Dubey, *SQL in a Week*, Apress Pocket Guides,
https://doi.org/10.1007/979-8-8688-2102-8_6

Why Optimization Matters

Badly written queries:

- Run slowly on large datasets

- Waste resources

- Are hard to maintain and debug

Well-optimized queries:

- Are **fast**, even at scale

- Use **fewer resources**

- Help your team work smarter, not harder

Use Indexes Wisely

Indexes speed up searches on columns used in WHERE, JOIN, and ORDER BY clauses.

Good example:

```
CREATE INDEX idx_employees_department ON
Employees(DepartmentID);
```

This helps when joining or filtering by department.

Avoid: Indexing every column. Indexes take up space and slow down writes (INSERT, UPDATE).

Avoid SELECT *

We've said it before, but it's worth repeating:

```
SELECT * FROM Employees;
```

fetches all columns—even if you only need two! This wastes bandwidth and processing.

Better:

```
SELECT FirstName, LastName FROM Employees;
```

Filter Early with WHERE

Apply filters as early as possible to reduce the rows SQL has to work with:

```
SELECT FirstName FROM Employees WHERE DepartmentID = 3;
```

This is much faster than filtering later in application code.

Use EXPLAIN to Analyze Query Plans

EXPLAIN shows how SQL will execute your query:

```
EXPLAIN SELECT * FROM Employees WHERE DepartmentID = 3;
```

Use it to understand if indexes are being used, where scans occur, and what can be optimized.

SQL Query Execution Order (What Runs First)

Even though we often write SQL starting with SELECT, the actual order in which SQL processes the query is different:

1. **FROM**: Determines the source tables and joins

2. **WHERE**: Filters rows from the data source

3. **GROUP BY**: Aggregates rows based on given columns

4. **HAVING**: Filters aggregated results

5. **SELECT**: Chooses which columns to return

6. **ORDER BY**: Sorts the final result

7. **LIMIT**: Restricts the number of output rows

Understanding this logical order helps you write more predictable and optimized queries, especially when using filters and aggregations.

Break Down Long Queries

Use **CTEs or temp tables** instead of giant monolithic queries. It's easier to test, debug, and optimize.

Use EXISTS Instead of IN (When Appropriate)

For large datasets, EXISTS can be more efficient than IN:

```
SELECT FirstName FROM Employees e WHERE EXISTS (SELECT 1 FROM
Departments d WHERE d.DepartmentID = e.DepartmentID);
```

See output in Figure 6-1.

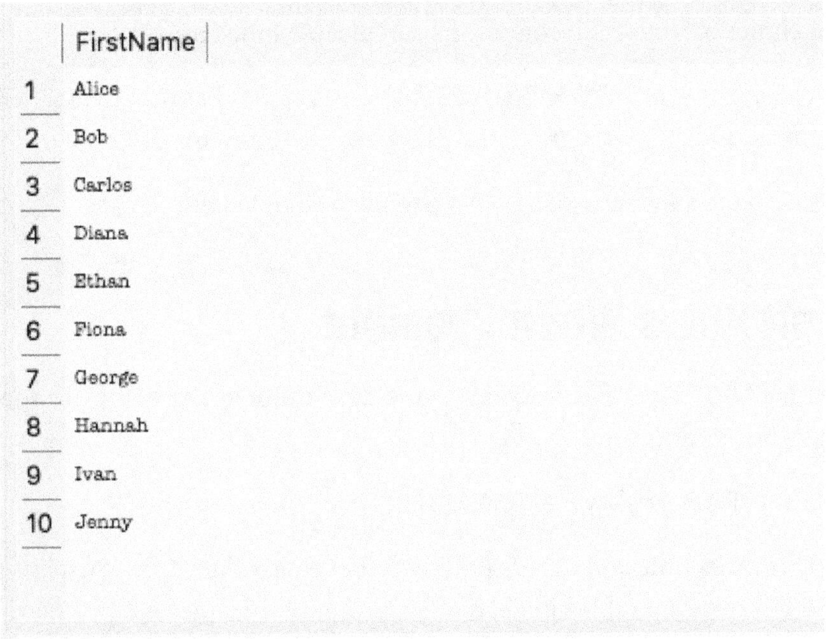

	FirstName
1	Alice
2	Bob
3	Carlos
4	Diana
5	Ethan
6	Fiona
7	George
8	Hannah
9	Ivan
10	Jenny

Figure 6-1. *Query Output*

This avoids scanning entire result sets when just a match is needed.

Watch for Implicit Conversions

If you're comparing mismatched data types, SQL might perform implicit conversions, slowing performance. Always ensure you're comparing compatible types:

```
-- Avoid this:WHERE EmployeeID = '123' -- EmployeeID is INT
-- Prefer this:WHERE EmployeeID = 123
```

Avoid Functions in WHERE Clauses

Using functions in WHERE conditions can disable index usage:

```
-- Avoid this:WHERE YEAR(HireDate) = 2023 -- Prefer this:WHERE
HireDate >= '2023-01-01' AND HireDate < '2024-01-01'
```

This allows indexes on HireDate to be used efficiently.

Limit Rows When Possible

Use LIMIT (or TOP in SQL Server) during development and testing to speed up query iteration:

```
SELECT * FROM Employees LIMIT 100;
```

This saves time and avoids pulling unnecessary data during trial runs. Use **CTEs or temp tables** instead of giant monolithic queries.

Key Takeaways

Concepts You Learned Today

- Why indexing matters and how to use it wisely

- Avoiding SELECT * to reduce data load

- Filtering early using WHERE

- Reading and interpreting query plans with EXPLAIN

- Writing modular queries for easier optimization

Best Practice of the Day

Test your queries with EXPLAIN and always write with scale in mind—think like your database is 100x bigger.

Common Mistake to Avoid

Don't rely on trial-and-error when queries are slow—learn to read execution plans and write with intent.

SQL in the Age of AI—AI and Optimization

- AI might write functional queries, but rarely efficient ones.

- Your knowledge of joins, indexes, and execution plans turns AI drafts into production-grade code.

- Performance is your job—AI is just the intern.

Coming Up on Saturday

It's almost graduation day! Tomorrow, we'll recap everything you've learned, go over **common SQL interview questions**, and give you tips to speak SQL fluently in your next big opportunity.

CHAPTER 7

Saturday: Graduation Day—Industry Smart and Interview Ready

Goal: Celebrate your journey through SQL mastery by recapping all the key concepts, providing a powerful review, and equipping you with **real interview questions**, **best practices**, and **final advice** to confidently enter the job market.

Saturday at DataNova Corp: From Learner to Leader

You did it, CEO! After a focused week learning SQL from the ground up, you've transformed into a data-savvy decision-maker. Today is about **reflection, revision, and readiness**.

Over the past week, you've evolved from writing your first SELECT statement to mastering joins, aggregations, CTEs, subqueries, window functions, and performance tuning. You've learned how to ask smart questions, retrieve meaningful answers, and speak the language of SQL like a pro. This final chapter is your bridge from learning SQL to confidently applying it in interviews, meetings, and real-world decision-making.

© Bhumika Shah and Devtosh Dubey 2026
B. Shah and D. Dubey, *SQL in a Week*, Apress Pocket Guides,
https://doi.org/10.1007/979-8-8688-2102-8_7

Translating Business Questions into SQL: A Practical Framework

As the CEO of DataNova Corp, you've probably noticed that many stakeholders—PMs, VPs, or even founders often don't speak SQL. That's okay. But *you* do now. SQL is the language of tables and columns, while business is the language of goals and decisions. Great data professionals bridge this gap. The more fluently you translate business questions into SQL queries and back, the more value you create. That's how data becomes action.

Understand the Business Goal First

Before even thinking in terms of SQL, get clarity on the "why." Business users often throw out vague requests like "Give me a report on sales." But what are they really asking? Is it to find top-selling products? Seasonal trends? Underperforming regions?

Therefore, Understanding the *intent* ensures your SQL query solves the actual business problem. Otherwise, you might write a perfect query that answers the wrong question.

Before writing any SQL, ask

- What decision will this data inform?

- What exactly do we want to know?

Example:

> *"We want to know which departments have underperforming employees."*

This may involve joining the Employees and Performance tables and filtering for low performance scores.

Break Down the Question into Data Elements

Breaking the problem into small parts makes the query easier to build, understand, and explain therefore to make it easy, users can use the classic W-W-W-W-W-H method (Who, What, When, Where, Why, and How) to map the business need to SQL terms like tables, columns, filters, and aggregations.

Use the W-W-W-W-W-H method:

- **What** data is needed? → Employee performance scores

- **Who** is involved? → Departments, employees

- **Where** is the data? → Which tables, which columns?

- **When** is the period of interest? → Filter on dates

- **Why** is this useful? → Helps plan training or restructuring

- **How** will we show this? → Columns, metrics, filters

Map Business Language to SQL Language

Many non-SQL users don't realize that SQL can group, filter, sort, and calculate. This mapping makes it easier to understand *what SQL is capable of.* Table 7-1 has some examples to translate business logic into SQL statements.

Table 7-1. *Translating business into SQL*

Business Term	SQL Equivalent
"Top-performing employees"	ORDER BY PerformanceScore DESC
"Employees in Europe"	WHERE Region = 'Europe'
"Departments with >5 people"	GROUP BY Department HAVING COUNT(employee) > 5
"Revenue by month"	GROUP BY MONTH(SaleDate)

Use SQL Comments to Clarify Intent

Comments help bridge the gap between technical SQL and business reasoning. They allow you to explain *why* a query exists—not just *what* it does—making your code more transparent and collaborative. In cross-functional teams like ours at DataNova, where engineers, analysts, and product owners work together, comments ensure that business logic isn't lost in translation.

They also reduce ambiguity during handoffs and code reviews, which is especially helpful when queries are revisited after weeks or months. And in the age of AI-assisted development, clear comments guide both human teammates and AI tools to generate, debug, or optimize queries with the correct intent.

Example:

```sql
-- Business Goal: List employees eligible for bonus (over $90k
salary, hired before 2021)
SELECT FirstName, LastName, Salary
FROM Employees
WHERE Salary > 90000 AND HireDate < '2021-01-01';
```

Think of comments as the CEO's note in the margin—short, clear, and full of business clarity.

Practice Reverse Translation: SQL to Business Speak

Not everyone reads SQL, but everyone understands insights. Translating back from SQL to business terms proves that you understand both the data and the story behind it. It shows you're not just a query writer—you're a decision enabler. The ability to map a table join to a real-world process, or turn filters into strategic priorities, is what separates a data executor from a data leader. Whether you're in the boardroom or at the command line, fluency in both languages—business and SQL—is your true superpower.

Example:

SQL:

```
SELECT d.DepartmentName, AVG(Salary) AS AvgSalary
FROM Employees e
JOIN Departments d on e.DepartmentID = d.DepartmentID
GROUP BY d.DepartmentName
ORDER BY AvgSalary DESC;
```

Business Summary:

"This tells us which departments have the highest average salaries. It helps us identify cost centers or plan budgets."

Bonus Tip: Use AI Tools, But Stay in Control

Tools like ChatGPT or Copilot can help generate SQL—but *you* must ensure the query aligns with business intent and filters data correctly. Think of AI as your copilot, not your decision-maker.

SQL Interview

You've spent an entire week diving deep into SQL—understanding, writing, and optimizing queries like a pro. Now, it's time to take that knowledge and prepare for one of the most important moments in your data journey: SQL interviews. Whether you're aiming for a data analyst role, a product-facing position, or a leadership spot where SQL fluency is a must, this chapter will help you bridge the gap between technical skill and real-world interview performance. Let's turn your hard-earned practice into confident answers.

What Interviewers Want to See

Interviewers don't just care about syntax. They're looking for someone who can solve business problems, someone who understands *why* a query is being written, *what* decision it's driving, and *how* to validate and communicate the results. Your ability to translate vague stakeholder questions into precise SQL logic is what sets you apart. It shows you're not just fluent in code but you're fluent in **context**, **data storytelling**, and **critical thinking**. That's the difference between a candidate who passes a coding round and one who *leads with data*.

- **Problem-Solving Approach:** Can you translate vague requirements into structured SQL?

- **Clarity and Correctness:** Are your joins, filters, and aggregations clean and purposeful?

- **Efficiency:** Are you avoiding unnecessary calculations and choosing the best logic path?

- **Communication:** Can you explain why you used a CTE or why LEFT JOIN makes sense here?

Essential Concepts to Master

Whether you're interviewing for a data analyst, business analyst, or product role, these are the core SQL areas you'll almost certainly be tested on (Table 7-2).

Table 7-2. *Interview tips*

Concept	Tip
Joins	Know when to use INNER, LEFT, FULL, and how NULLs behave
Aggregations	Use GROUP BY, HAVING, and be ready to calculate metrics like average revenue per user
Window Functions	Especially ROW_NUMBER, RANK, LAG, and LEAD for time-series or deduplication problems
Subqueries	Useful for filtering or checking existence (EXISTS, IN, NOT IN)
CTEs	Use WITH to write readable queries, especially multi-step logic
Filters	Understand the difference between WHERE vs HAVING
Optimization	Avoid SELECT *, use indexed columns, filter early, and write readable logic
Debugging	Read your query step-by-step and validate outputs incrementally

SQL Interview Questions You Should Be Ready For

Efficient SQL writing isn't just about getting the syntax right but it's about understanding the *why* behind each clause. Choosing INNER JOIN over OUTER JOIN, using HAVING instead of WHERE, or indexing the right column can make the difference between a slow, unreadable query and a performant, scalable solution. This level of understanding is what separates a beginner from a professional and it is exactly what interviewers are looking for.

Beginner to Intermediate

1. **What is the difference between INNER JOIN, LEFT JOIN, and FULL JOIN?**

   INNER JOIN returns only matching rows from both tables.

   LEFT JOIN returns all rows from the left table, plus matching rows from the right table (if any).

   FULL JOIN returns all rows from both tables, with NULL where there's no match.

2. **How does GROUP BY differ from ORDER BY?**

   GROUP BY is used to group rows for aggregate functions like SUM() or COUNT().

   ORDER BY is used to sort the results by one or more columns, either ascending or descending.

   They serve different purposes and can be used together.

3. **What is a NULL value and how do you handle it?**

   A NULL represents missing or unknown data.

   You handle it using IS NULL, IS NOT NULL, or functions like COALESCE() to replace it with a default.

   NULLs don't behave like regular values in comparisons (e.g., NULL != NULL is unknown).

4. **What is a subquery and where can you use it?**

   A subquery is a query inside another query, enclosed in parentheses.

You can use it in SELECT, FROM, or WHERE clauses.

Subqueries help break complex problems into manageable parts.

5. **Explain the purpose of the HAVING clause.**

   HAVING filters groups after aggregation (e.g., after using GROUP BY).

   Use it to filter based on SUM(), AVG(), etc.

   Unlike WHERE, it works on grouped (aggregated) results.

6. **How do you find duplicate rows in a table?**

```
SELECT column1, COUNT(*)
FROM table
GROUP BY column1
HAVING COUNT(*) > 1;
--This groups by a column and returns any values that
appear more than once.
```

Intermediate to Advanced

1. **What is the difference between RANK() and ROW_NUMBER()?**

   ROW_NUMBER() gives a unique number to each row, even if there's a tie.

   RANK() assigns the same rank to tied rows but skips the next number(s).

   Useful for pagination, leaderboards, or partitioning data.

2. **Explain the difference between WHERE and HAVING.**

   WHERE filters rows **before** grouping.

   HAVING filters aggregated data **after** grouping.

   Both are essential but used at different stages in query execution.

3. **When would you use CROSS APPLY instead of a JOIN?**

   CROSS APPLY is used when the right-side table or function depends on the left-side row.

   It's often used with table-valued functions.

   A JOIN doesn't support this row-by-row dependency.

4. **What are the different types of physical joins and when are they used?**

   Nested Loop: Great for small datasets

   Merge Join: Efficient for sorted data

   Hash Join: Used when there's no index or sorting—good for large, unsorted data

   These impact performance and are chosen by the SQL engine.

5. **How do isolation levels affect concurrency and data consistency?**

   Isolation levels control how transactions interact.

Levels like READ COMMITTED, REPEATABLE READ, and SERIALIZABLE prevent issues like dirty reads or phantom reads.

Higher levels improve consistency but may reduce concurrency.

6. **What is the difference between EXISTS and IN?**

   EXISTS checks if a subquery returns **any rows**.

   IN checks if a value exists **in a list**.

   EXISTS is faster for correlated subqueries; IN works better for static lists.

7. **What is an execution plan and how do you use it?**

   An execution plan shows how SQL Server will run your query (e.g., which indexes it uses).

   Use it to find performance bottlenecks.

   In SSMS, click "Display Estimated Execution Plan" to see it.

8. **Explain the difference between SCOPE_ IDENTITY() and @@IDENTITY.**

   SCOPE_IDENTITY() returns the last identity value in the current scope (safe for triggers).

   @@IDENTITY returns the last identity value across all scopes, including triggers.

   Use SCOPE_IDENTITY() to avoid unexpected results.

Tips for Acing SQL Interviews So That the Interviewer Picks You Out of Everyone

- **Share Your Query Plan with Interviewer**: Always clarify the business question before writing SQL.

- **Ask Questions from Interviewer**: Ask for sample data or expected output to guide your query.

- **Start Simple**: Start with simple queries like Select Column from table, and refine for performance.

- **Use Aliases**: Use meaningful aliases with tables and columns and avoid `SELECT *`.

- **Speak Your Logic**: Speak through your logic clearly while writing the query.

- **Communicate Your Story**: When stuck, narrate what you're thinking—interviewers value reasoning.

- **Practice**: Practice SQL challenges on platforms like LeetCode, HackerRank, and StrataScratch.

Final Advice from the Author

SQL is not just a query language—it's a way of thinking. Like any language, the more you practice, the more fluent and confident you become.

You've done something amazing this week. From installing your first database to mastering optimization, you're now equipped with both the **syntax and the strategy** of SQL. Go out there, lead your data teams, nail those interviews, and don't forget—

Write with clarity. Query with purpose. Think like a CEO.

CHAPTER 8

Bonus: Industry Best Practices and Next Steps

Kudos, CEO. You did it.

In just seven days, you went from writing your first SELECT statement to understanding joins, aggregations, window functions, optimization techniques, and even preparing for SQL interviews. That's no small accomplishment.

But as every leader at DataNova knows, learning a skill is only the beginning. The real test begins when you start applying that knowledge to real business questions.

At DataNova Corp, questions rarely come neatly packaged as textbook exercises. Instead, your team might ask

- Which departments are growing the fastest?

- Are we over or under-utilizing our employees this week?

- Which projects are burning through budget faster than expected?

- Are teams collaborating effectively across locations and departments?

B. Shah and D. Dubey, *SQL in a Week*, Apress Pocket Guides,
https://doi.org/10.1007/979-8-8688-2102-8_8

Each of these questions requires more than just writing a simple query. They require combining multiple SQL concepts, thinking about business logic, and structuring queries that reveal meaningful insights.

In this bonus section, you will tackle a set of practical SQL problems inspired by real-world analytics scenarios. For each question, we will first explain the business problem, outline the strategy for solving it, and then walk through the SQL solution step by step.

Think of these exercises as your **final leadership briefing as the CEO of DataNova**—where data becomes strategy, and SQL becomes the language that powers decisions.

Let's begin with the first challenge.

Q1) Department Headcount and Median Salary

Question: For each department, return headcount and **median** salary.

```
-- Goal: Headcount and median salary per department in SQLite
(no built-in MEDIAN).
-- Strategy:
--    1) Rank salaries ascending and descending within each
department.
--    2) Identify the "middle" row(s) using integer math:
mid1=(n+1)/2, mid2=(n+2)/2.
--    3) Average the middle row(s) to get the median (works for
odd/even n).
WITH ranked AS (
  SELECT
    d.DepartmentID,
    d.DepartmentName,
    e.Salary,
```

```
    ROW_NUMBER() OVER (PARTITION BY d.DepartmentID ORDER BY
    e.Salary)          AS rn_asc,
    ROW_NUMBER() OVER (PARTITION BY d.DepartmentID ORDER BY
    e.Salary DESC)   AS rn_desc,
    COUNT(*)         OVER (PARTITION BY d.Department
    ID)                           AS n
  FROM Departments d
  JOIN Employees    e ON e.DepartmentID = d.DepartmentID
),
middle AS (
  SELECT
    DepartmentID,
    DepartmentName,
    Salary,
    n,
    ((n + 1) / 2) AS mid1,    -- integer division ->
    floor((n+1)/2)
    ((n + 2) / 2) AS mid2,    -- integer division ->
    ceil((n+1)/2)
    rn_asc,
    rn_desc
  FROM ranked
)
SELECT
  DepartmentID,
  DepartmentName,
  COUNT(*)       AS headcount,
  AVG(Salary)    AS median_salary  -- average one or two
  middle rows
```

```
FROM middle
WHERE rn_asc IN (mid1, mid2)
  AND rn_desc IN (mid1, mid2)
GROUP BY DepartmentID, DepartmentName
ORDER BY DepartmentID;
```

See output in Figure 8-1.

	DepartmentID	DepartmentName	headcount	median_salary
1	1	Marketing	2	71800.0
2	2	Engineering	2	97500.0
3	3	HR	2	66000.0
4	4	Support	2	59500.0

Figure 8-1. *Query Output*

Q2) Planned vs. Actual Hours (Weekly Utilization)

Question: For a given week (e.g., 2023-06-12), compare planned vs. actual hours per employee.

```
-- Param: :week_start (e.g., '2023-06-12')
-- planned = SUM of HoursPerWeek across all assignments
(static per employee)
-- actual  = SUM of Timesheets.Hours for that week
```

```
WITH planned AS (
  SELECT a.EmployeeID, SUM(a.HoursPerWeek) AS planned_hours
  FROM Assignments a
  GROUP BY a.EmployeeID
),
actual AS (
  SELECT t.EmployeeID, SUM(t.Hours) AS actual_hours
  FROM Timesheets t
  WHERE t.WeekStart = :week_start
  GROUP BY t.EmployeeID
)
SELECT
  e.EmployeeID,
  e.FirstName || ' ' || e.LastName AS EmployeeName,
  COALESCE(p.planned_hours, 0) AS planned_hours,
  COALESCE(a.actual_hours, 0)  AS actual_hours,
  COALESCE(a.actual_hours, 0) - COALESCE(p.planned_hours, 0) AS
delta_hours
FROM Employees e
LEFT JOIN planned p ON p.EmployeeID = e.EmployeeID
LEFT JOIN actual  a ON a.EmployeeID = e.EmployeeID
ORDER BY delta_hours DESC, EmployeeName;
```

See output in Figure 8-2.

	EmployeeID	EmployeeName	planned_hours	actual_hours	delta_hours
1	6	Fiona Davis	12	0	-12
2	3	Carlos Ramirez	15	0	-15
3	8	Hannah Zhang	18	0	-18
4	1	Alice Johnson	20	0	-20
5	9	Ivan Petrov	20	0	-20
6	4	Diana Wang	25	0	-25
7	7	George Clark	25	0	-25
8	10	Jenny Nguyen	28	0	-28
9	5	Ethan Kim	30	0	-30
10	2	Bob Lee	35	0	-35

Figure 8-2. *Query Output*

Q3) Budget Burn Variance (June 2023)

Question: For June 2023, compare planned vs. actual monthly hours and compute variance % per project.

```
-- Assumption: 1 month ≈ 4 weeks, so planned_month =
   SUM(HoursPerWeek) * 4.
-- Actuals are summed for weeks with WeekStart in June 2023.

WITH planned AS (
  SELECT a.ProjectID, SUM(a.HoursPerWeek) * 4.0 AS planned_
  hours_month
  FROM Assignments a
  GROUP BY a.ProjectID
),
```

```
actual AS (
  SELECT t.ProjectID, SUM(t.Hours) AS actual_hours_month
  FROM Timesheets t
  WHERE t.WeekStart >= '2023-06-01' AND t.WeekStart <
  '2023-07-01'
  GROUP BY t.ProjectID
)
SELECT
  p.ProjectID,
  p.ProjectName,
  COALESCE(pl.planned_hours_month, 0) AS planned_hours,
  COALESCE(ac.actual_hours_month, 0)  AS actual_hours,
  CASE
    WHEN COALESCE(pl.planned_hours_month, 0) = 0 THEN NULL
    ELSE (COALESCE(ac.actual_hours_month, 0) - pl.planned_
    hours_month) * 100.0
        / pl.planned_hours_month
  END AS variance_pct
FROM Projects p
LEFT JOIN planned pl ON pl.ProjectID = p.ProjectID
LEFT JOIN actual  ac ON ac.ProjectID = p.ProjectID
-- Emulate NULLS LAST by sorting on a boolean key first
ORDER BY (variance_pct IS NULL) ASC, variance_pct DESC,
p.ProjectID;
```

See output in Figure 8-3.

	ProjectID	ProjectName	planned_hours	actual_hours	variance_pct
1	102	AI Chatbot	200.0	96	-52.0
2	108	Ticket System Revamp	80.0	38	-52.5
3	106	Cloud Migration	272.0	127	-53.3088235294118
4	101	Brand Redesign	40.0	18	-55.0
5	105	Product Launch	88.0	22	-75.0
6	103	Recruitment Drive	60.0	0	-100.0
7	104	Helpdesk Upgrade	100.0	0	-100.0
8	107	Employee Onboarding	72.0	0	-100.0

Figure 8-3. *Query Output*

Q4) Location Diversity Index

Question: For each project, find the dominant (mode) employee location and the % of team outside it.

```
-- Steps:
-- 1) roster: (Project, Employee, Location).
-- 2) location_counts: per-project counts per location.
-- 3) mode_location: pick the location with highest count
      (FIRST_VALUE over counts).
-- 4) diversity: count team members not in the dominant
      location; compute %.

WITH roster AS (
  SELECT a.ProjectID, e.EmployeeID, e.Location
  FROM Assignments a
  JOIN Employees   e ON e.EmployeeID = a.EmployeeID
),
```

```sql
location_counts AS (
  SELECT ProjectID, Location, COUNT(*) AS loc_count
  FROM roster
  GROUP BY ProjectID, Location
),
mode_location AS (
  SELECT
    ProjectID,
    FIRST_VALUE(Location) OVER (
      PARTITION BY ProjectID
      ORDER BY loc_count DESC, Location
    ) AS mode_loc,
    SUM(loc_count) OVER (PARTITION BY ProjectID) AS
    total_people
  FROM location_counts
),
diversity AS (
  SELECT
    r.ProjectID,
    ml.mode_loc,
    ml.total_people,
    SUM(CASE WHEN r.Location <> ml.mode_loc THEN 1 ELSE 0 END)
    AS off_mode_count
  FROM roster r
  JOIN mode_location ml ON ml.ProjectID = r.ProjectID
  GROUP BY r.ProjectID, ml.mode_loc, ml.total_people
)
SELECT
  d.ProjectID,
  p.ProjectName,
  d.mode_loc AS DominantLocation,
```

```
  d.total_people AS TeamSize,
  d.off_mode_count AS OffModeCount,
  CASE WHEN d.total_people = 0 THEN 0.0
       ELSE d.off_mode_count * 100.0 / d.total_people END AS
       pct_off_dominant_location
FROM diversity d
JOIN Projects p ON p.ProjectID = d.ProjectID
ORDER BY pct_off_dominant_location DESC, d.ProjectID;
```

See output in Figure 8-4.

	ProjectID	ProjectName	DominantLocation	TeamSize	OffModeCount	pct_off_dominant_location
1	102	AI Chatbot	San Francisco	2	2	100.0
2	106	Cloud Migration	San Francisco	3	2	66.6666666666667
3	101	Brand Redesign	New York	1	0	0.0
4	103	Recruitment Drive	London	1	0	0.0
5	104	Helpdesk Upgrade	Bangalore	1	0	0.0
6	105	Product Launch	New York	2	0	0.0
7	107	Employee Onboarding	London	1	0	0.0
8	108	Ticket System Revamp	Bangalore	1	0	0.0

Figure 8-4. *Query Output*

Q5) Cross-Department Collaboration

Question: For each department, count distinct other departments it collaborates with on the same projects.

```
-- Definition: Two departments "collaborate" if both staff the
   same project.
-- Steps:
--    proj_depts: distinct (ProjectID, DepartmentID).
--    pairs: for each project, all ordered pairs of two
       different departments (use < to avoid dup/self).
```

```sql
--    rollup: make the relation symmetric by UNION ALL.
--    Final: count distinct OtherDept per Department.

WITH proj_depts AS (
  SELECT DISTINCT a.ProjectID, e.DepartmentID
  FROM Assignments a
  JOIN Employees   e ON e.EmployeeID = a.EmployeeID
),
pairs AS (
  SELECT pd1.DepartmentID AS dept_a, pd2.DepartmentID AS dept_b
  FROM proj_depts pd1
  JOIN proj_depts pd2
    ON pd1.ProjectID = pd2.ProjectID
   AND pd1.DepartmentID < pd2.DepartmentID
),
rollup AS (
  SELECT dept_a AS DepartmentID, dept_b AS OtherDept FROM pairs
  UNION ALL
  SELECT dept_b AS DepartmentID, dept_a AS OtherDept FROM pairs
)
SELECT
  d.DepartmentID,
  d.DepartmentName,
  COUNT(DISTINCT r.OtherDept) AS CollaboratingDepartments
FROM Departments d
LEFT JOIN rollup r ON r.DepartmentID = d.DepartmentID
GROUP BY d.DepartmentID, d.DepartmentName
ORDER BY CollaboratingDepartments DESC, d.DepartmentID;
```

See output in Figure 8-5.

	DepartmentID	DepartmentName	CollaboratingDepartments
1	1	Marketing	0
2	2	Engineering	0
3	3	HR	0
4	4	Support	0

Figure 8-5. *Query Output*

Q6) Latest Salary vs. Current Salary Alignment

Question: Show each employee's latest SalaryChanges.NewSalary and whether it matches Employees.Salary.

```
-- Use ROW_NUMBER() to select the most recent change per
employee.
-- Output IsAligned as 1/0 to keep SQLite-friendly boolean.

WITH latest AS (
  SELECT
    sc.EmployeeID,
    sc.NewSalary,
    sc.EffectiveDate,
    ROW_NUMBER() OVER (
      PARTITION BY sc.EmployeeID
      ORDER BY sc.EffectiveDate DESC
    ) AS rn
  FROM SalaryChanges sc
)
```

```
SELECT
  e.EmployeeID,
  e.FirstName || ' ' || e.LastName AS EmployeeName,
  l.NewSalary     AS LatestSalaryChange,
  e.Salary        AS EmployeeSalary,
  l.EffectiveDate AS LatestEffectiveDate,
  CASE WHEN l.NewSalary IS NOT NULL AND e.Salary = l.NewSalary
THEN 1 ELSE 0 END AS IsAligned
FROM Employees e
LEFT JOIN latest l
  ON l.EmployeeID = e.EmployeeID AND l.rn = 1
ORDER BY IsAligned ASC, l.EffectiveDate DESC, e.EmployeeID;
```

See output in Figure 8-6.

	EmployeeID	EmployeeName	LatestSalaryChange	EmployeeSalary	LatestEffectiveDate	IsAligned
1	3	Carlos Ramirez	NULL	65000	NULL	0
2	4	Diana Wang	NULL	60000	NULL	0
3	6	Fiona Davis	NULL	71000	NULL	0
4	8	Hannah Zhang	NULL	67000	NULL	0
5	9	Ivan Petrov	NULL	59000	NULL	0
6	10	Jenny Nguyen	NULL	97000	NULL	0
7	1	Alice Johnson	72000	72000	2023-04-01	1
8	2	Bob Lee	95000	95000	2022-08-01	1
9	5	Ethan Kim	98000	98000	2022-05-01	1
10	7	George Clark	105000	105000	2021-03-01	1

Figure 8-6. *Query Output*

Q7) High-Salary Employees on Low-Budget Projects

Question: List employees earning ≥ their department average who are on projects with budget < 100000.

```
-- Step 1: Compute average salary per department.
-- Step 2: Join to assignments/projects and filter on salary
   and budget thresholds.

WITH dept_avg AS (
  SELECT DepartmentID, AVG(Salary) AS dept_avg_salary
  FROM Employees
  GROUP BY DepartmentID
)
SELECT DISTINCT
  e.EmployeeID,
  e.FirstName || ' ' || e.LastName AS EmployeeName,
  d.DepartmentName,
  e.Salary,
  p.ProjectID,
  p.ProjectName,
  p.Budget
FROM Employees    e
JOIN dept_avg    da ON da.DepartmentID = e.DepartmentID
JOIN Departments d  ON d.DepartmentID = e.DepartmentID
JOIN Assignments a  ON a.EmployeeID   = e.EmployeeID
JOIN Projects    p  ON p.ProjectID    = a.ProjectID
WHERE e.Salary >= da.dept_avg_salary
  AND p.Budget < 100000
ORDER BY d.DepartmentName, e.Salary DESC, p.Budget ASC,
p.ProjectID;
```

See output in Figure 8-7.

	EmployeeID	EmployeeName	DepartmentName	Salary	ProjectID	ProjectName	Budget
1	8	Hannah Zhang	HR	67000	107	Employee Onboarding	95000
2	4	Diana Wang	Support	60000	104	Helpdesk Upgrade	60000

Figure 8-7. *Query Output*

Q8) Department Budget Concentration

Question: For each department, compute the % of budget in its single largest project.

```
-- Steps:
--    1) dept_proj: list of projects with budgets by department.
--    2) dept_totals: total budget per department.
--    3) ranked: DENSE_RANK projects by budget within
         department.
--    4) Pick rnk=1 and compute share% = top_project_budget /
         department_total.

WITH dept_proj AS (
  SELECT p.DepartmentID, p.ProjectID, p.ProjectName, p.Budget
  FROM Projects p
),
dept_totals AS (
  SELECT DepartmentID, SUM(Budget) AS dept_budget_total
  FROM dept_proj
  GROUP BY DepartmentID
),
ranked AS (
  SELECT
    dp.*,
    dt.dept_budget_total,
```

```
    DENSE_RANK() OVER (
      PARTITION BY dp.DepartmentID
      ORDER BY dp.Budget DESC, dp.ProjectID
    ) AS rnk
  FROM dept_proj dp
  JOIN dept_totals dt ON dt.DepartmentID = dp.DepartmentID
)
SELECT
  d.DepartmentID,
  d.DepartmentName,
  r.ProjectID,
  r.ProjectName,
  r.Budget            AS TopProjectBudget,
  r.dept_budget_total AS DeptBudgetTotal,
  CASE WHEN r.dept_budget_total = 0 THEN 0.0
      ELSE r.Budget * 100.0 / r.dept_budget_total END AS
      TopProjectSharePct
FROM ranked r
JOIN Departments d ON d.DepartmentID = r.DepartmentID
WHERE r.rnk = 1
ORDER BY TopProjectSharePct DESC, d.DepartmentID;
```

See output in Figure 8-8.

	DepartmentID	DepartmentName	ProjectID	ProjectName	TopProjectBudget	DeptBudgetTotal	TopProjectSharePct
1	1	Marketing	105	Product Launch	200000	350000	57.1428571428571
2	2	Engineering	106	Cloud Migration	400000	700000	57.1428571428571
3	4	Support	108	Ticket System Revamp	75000	135000	55.5555555555556
4	3	HR	107	Employee Onboarding	95000	175000	54.2857142857143

Figure 8-8. *Query Output*

Congratulations, Graduate!

You're now ready to

- Build efficient, optimized queries

- Interpret and clean real-world data

- Solve business problems with SQL logic

- Stand out in technical interviews

Welcome to the data world—you speak its favorite language, SQL, now!

Disclaimer

SQLite is a public domain relational database engine used in this book for educational and practice purposes. SQLite is not affiliated with or endorsing this publication.

GPSR Compliance
The European Union's (EU) General Product Safety Regulation (GPSR) is a set
of rules that requires consumer products to be safe and our obligations to
ensure this.

If you have any concerns about our products, you can contact us on

ProductSafety@springernature.com

In case Publisher is established outside the EU, the EU authorized
representative is:

Springer Nature Customer Service Center GmbH
Europaplatz 3
69115 Heidelberg, Germany